SADLIER
FAITH AND
WITNESS

New Testament

A Course on Jesus Christ and His Disciples

Norman F. Josaitis, S. T. D.

Rev. Michael J. Lanning, O. F. M.

Special Consultant
Mary Ann Getty, S. T. D.

William H. Sadlier, Inc.
9 Pine Street
New York, New York 10005-1002
www.sadlier.com

Acknowledgments

Scripture selections are taken from the *New American Bible* Copyright © 1991, 1986, 1970 by the Confraternity of Christian Doctrine, Washington, D.C. and are used by license of the copyright owner. All rights reserved. No part of the *New American Bible* may be used or reproduced in any form, without permission in writing from the copyright owner.

Excerpts from the English translation of the *Catechism of the Catholic Church* for use in the United States of America, Copyright © 1994, United States Catholic Conference, Inc.—Libreria Editrice Vaticana.

Excerpts from the English translation of *Lectionary for Mass* © 1969, International Committee on English in the Liturgy, Inc. (ICEL); excerpts from the English translation of *The Roman Missal* © 1973, ICEL; excerpts from the English translation of *Book of Blessings* © 1988, ICEL. All rights reserved.

English translation of the Canticle of Zechariah (Benedictus), Canticle of Mary (Magnificat), Canticle of Simeon (Nunc Dimittis) by the International Consultation on English Texts, (ICET).

Extract from the poem "As Kingfishers catch fire . . ." Gerard Manley Hopkins, Oxford University Press.

Excerpt from *The Documents of Vatican II*, Walter M. Abbott, S.J., General Editor, © 1966 by America Press, Inc.

Cover Illustrator: David Diaz
Map Illustrator: Mapping Specialists, Ltd.

Photo Credits

Ancient Art and Architecture: 21, 48.
Art Resource/ 177 bottom; Alinari: 10; Victoria and Albert Museum, London: 12–13; The Pierpont Morgan Library: 14; Nicolo Orsi Battaglini: 24; D.Y.: 72 top, 73 bottom, 74 bottom, 75 top; Scala: 81, 82, 174 top, 174 bottom, 175 right center, 175 left top, 180 top, 184, 185 left, 185 bottom; Murillo: 86; Giraudon: 175 left center; Bildarchive Foto Marburg: 175 bottom; Erich Lessing: 178 left, 181 bottom right, 182; Tate Gallery, London: 130, 179 top left.
Scott Barrow: 162–163 hands.
Boltin Picture Library: 178 right.
Brainworks/ Michelle Kahn: 155 hands.
Bridgeman Art Library, London/ New York: Guildhall Art Gallery, Corporation of London: 62, 183 top; Birmingham Museum and Art Gallery: 180 bottom; National Gallery of Scotland, Edinburgh: 181 center; National Gallery of Ireland, Dublin: 183 center left.
Bridge Building Images: 179 top right.
Canadian Catholic Conference, Ottawa, Canada/ Thomas E. Moore: 176.
Corbis: 177 top.
Crosiers/ Gene Plaisted, OSC: 94, 140–141, 155(all stained glass), 165, 169, 174 right, 175.
Detroit Institute of Art: 85.
FPG/ Stephen Simpson: 9; JP Fruchet: 120; Steven Jones: 134–135; Burgess Blevins: 156 right; Telegraph Colour Library: 156 left.
Granger Collection: 147.
Image Bank/ Will Crocker: 20; Petrified Collection: 46; Mark Romanelli: 116; Kauko Helavuo: 167.
Image Works/ Chapman: 166.
Ken Karp: 47.
Liasion International/ Baitel–Kires: 59; Annie Assouline: 63; Quidu: 66–67.
The Metropolitan Museum of Art/ H.O. Havemeyer Collection, Bequest of Mrs. H.O. Havemeyer, 1929 (29.107.7): 179 bottom; Bequest of Benjamin Altman, 1913 (14.40.631): 185 top.
Museum der Bildenden Kunste: 181 top.

National Gallery of Art, Washington/ Samuel H. Kress Collection: 142.
National Geographic/ Paul Chesley: 114–115.
Natural Exposures/ Daniel Cox: 32, 33.
Natural Selection: 108–109, 118; Orion Press: 104–105.
Richard Nowitz: 50, 51, 56–57, 60 background, 61, 92, 132, 134.
Palm Beach Post/ Bob Shandley: 84.
Photographers Aspen/ Paul Chesley: 170–171.
Photonica/ K. Nagasawa: 30–31; H. Kuwajima: 80; Allen Wallace: 143.
Photo Researchers/ Allan Morton and Dennis Milon: 36; John Foster: 37; Mike Agliolo: 54–55.
Picture Perfect: 78–79.
Prints For Inspiration: 152.
Greg Probst: 6–7.
Questar: 60 foreground.
Santa Barbara Museum of Art/ Scott McClaine, Gift of Mrs. Sterling Morton to the Preston Morton Collection: 128.
Sisters of the Mississippi Abbey: 49.
Stock Imagery/ Powers: 18–19; Katz: 24–25; Stacks: 98 sky; Share: 98 prayer; Aika: 122; Russell: 126–127, 164.
Stock Market/ José Fuste Raga: 90–91.
Superstock: 8, 10–11, 68, 72 bottom, 73 top, 74 top, 75 bottom, 96.
Sygma/ Gianni Giansanti: 138–139.
Tony Stone Images: 102–103; Jonathan Morgan: 22 man; Glen Allison: 22 volcano; Stephen Johnson: 23; Earth Imaging: 26; Wayne Eastep: 34; David Young– Wolff: 35; I. Burgam/P. Boorman: 38–39; Will and Deni McIntyre: 38; David Austen: 42–43; Rohan: 58; Camille Tokerud: 70; Demetrio Carrasco: 87; Anton Want: 117; Lois and Bob Schlowsky: 129; Ed Honowitz: 145; Robert Frerck: 146; Andrew Syred: 150–151; Mark Lewis: 151; David Oliver: 158; Mike Magnuson: 162–163 clouds; Simon Norfolk: 168 left; David Job: 168 top; Andrea Booher: 168 right; John Turner 170–171 clouds.
Westlight/ Digital Art: 69; Robert Landau: 107, 110–111.
Bill Wittman: 27, 144, 156 top, 157.

General Consultant
Rev. Joseph A. Komonchak, Ph.D.

Official Theological Consultant
Most Rev. Edward K. Braxton, Ph.D., S.T.D.
Auxiliary Bishop of St. Louis

Publisher
Gerard F. Baumbach, Ed.D.

Editor in Chief
Moya Gullage

Pastoral Consultant
Rev. Msgr. John F. Barry

Scriptural Consultant
Rev. Donald Senior, C.P., Ph.D., S.T.D.

General Editors
Norman F. Josaitis, S.T.D.
Rev. Michael J. Lanning, O.F.M.

Catechetical and Liturgical Consultants
Eleanor Ann Brownell, D.Min.
Joseph F. Sweeney
Helen Hemmer, I.H.M.
Mary Frances Hession
Maureen Sullivan, O.P., Ph.D.
Don Boyd

"The Ad Hoc Committee to Oversee the Use of the Catechism,
National Conference of Catholic Bishops,
has found this catechetical text to be in conformity
with the *Catechism of the Catholic Church*."

Nihil Obstat
✠ Most Reverend George O. Wirz
Censor Librorum

Imprimatur
✠ Most Reverend William H. Bullock
Bishop of Madison
May 20, 1998

The *Nihil Obstat* and *Imprimatur* are official
declarations that a book or pamphlet is free of
doctrinal or moral error. No implication is contained
therein that those who have granted the *Nihil Obstat*
and *Imprimatur* agree with the contents, opinions, or
statements expressed.

Printed in the United States of America.

S is a registered trademark of William H. Sadlier, Inc.

Home Office:
9 Pine Street
New York, NY 10005–1002

ISBN: 8215-5601-0
121314151617/10 09 08 07 06

Unlike Any Other

Ask and you will receive; seek and you will find; knock and the door will be opened to you.

Luke 11:9

Do you remember what it was like when you were very young and were learning to swim? What do you remember most, and why?

Deeper Water

When parents bring their young children to the beach to go swimming, they do not send them out to the deep water right away. That would be frightening to the children and perhaps dangerous. Instead children need to get used to the water gradually. Only after they have become comfortable in the water and enjoy it will they learn to swim. Only then can they venture out and experience the excitement of deeper water.

Many things in our lives can be compared to the experience of going out into deep water. For example, we cannot get a real education until we know how to read. We cannot explore cyberspace until we know something about computers. We cannot excel in a game or a sport until we have mastered the rules.

In many ways the same can be said about our life of faith. When we were little children, we were introduced to the beauty of our Catholic faith. We began to learn the basics of our religion at the appropriate age level. Once that was done, we could begin to practice our faith and come to know God in our lives. But now it is time for a change. It is time to go out into deeper water.

Jesus himself once invited some people to "put out into deep water" (Luke 5:4). These people were fishermen. They had been working hard fishing all night long but had been unsuccessful in catching anything. When they answered Jesus' invitation, something wonderful happened. They caught more fish than their nets could hold. Once the fishermen saw this, they left everything and followed him.

In a wonderful way Jesus is inviting you now to put out into deep water, too. He is the center of our faith, and he wants you to know him in a deeper and more mature way. Jesus wants you to come closer to him than you have ever been before. He wants you to explore the questions you have about him, about his life and teachings, and about following him in your life.

The invitation might seem almost overwhelming. How can a person even begin to respond to it? To do this, people for the last twenty centuries and in all parts of the world have turned to the Church. After all, it was Jesus who founded the Church and who sent the Holy Spirit upon it. Today it is through the Church that we experience Jesus and learn about him.

For the Church "the key, the center, and the purpose of the whole of man's history is to be found in its Lord and Master" (*Catechism of the Catholic Church,* 450). By being faithful members of the Church, we are able to respond to Jesus' invitation and come closer to him. We hear the story of Jesus and begin to live the good news that he came to share with us. This good news comes to us in Sacred Scripture and in the Church's living witness and tradition.

Knowing all about the good news of Jesus is more than the work of one lifetime! The purpose of this book is to help us enter more deeply into one part of Sacred Scripture, the New Testament. Catholics who participate in Mass and have attended religion classes have already been introduced to the New Testament. But now it is time to plunge into it more deeply.

Will we learn everything about the New Testament? That would be impossible! Some scholars spend a lifetime studying one part of the New Testament and never exhaust what can be found there. They learn the original language spoken by Jesus and travel to the places where he lived and walked. They do this so that we might have a clearer understanding of Jesus and what he means for us and for the world. In this course some of their discoveries will become ours.

We are about to launch out into the deeper water of the New Testament. Are you ready to plunge in?

 What is the one question you have always wanted to ask Jesus about his life? Write it in your journal.

The Truth from Outside

We are going to spend the rest of this chapter and the next few chapters on background material for our study of the New Testament. Several important questions need to be asked. Chief among these questions is: Did Jesus really exist at all? How do we answer this question? What proof do we have outside of the New Testament and the testimony of the Church?

Actually a number of nonbiblical and non-Christian written sources are available to anyone who wishes to read them. They verify the fact that Jesus of Nazareth was a historical figure. He lived in a small country on the eastern shores of the Mediterranean Sea. This was the land of the Jews, and Jesus himself was a Jew. At the time of his birth, his country was a part of the Roman Empire. In fact both the Romans and the Jews give witness to his existence.

One ancient Roman writer was named Pliny the Younger (A.D. 61–113). He was a Roman governor in a province of Asia Minor and was a great letter writer. In one of his letters, he asked the advice of the Roman emperor Trajan on dealing with a religious group called Christians. In the course of the letter, Pliny mentioned that Christianity was causing the revenue from pagan temples and shrines to decline. Because these temples and shrines were being used less and less, the animals used for sacrifice were not being sold. He told the emperor that he was trying to get the Christians to reject Jesus Christ and to accept the pagan gods of the empire. If the Christians continued to profess their faith in Jesus, Pliny said that he would have to put them to death.

In his letter of response, Trajan praised Pliny for the way he was handling the Christian problem. Like Pliny, Trajan did not say much about Jesus himself, but he presumed that Jesus existed because he had so many followers.

Another ancient Roman writer was Tacitus (about A.D. 56–120). He was a historian and wrote about many things, including the great fire that happened in Rome during the reign of the emperor Nero. Although Nero himself probably started the fire, he successfully blamed the Christians for burning the city and put many of them to death. Writing about Nero and the fire, Tacitus said of the Christians, "Their name comes from Christ, who, during the reign of Tiberius, had been executed by the procurator Pontius Pilate" (*Annals*, 15, 44).

Detail from painting of Christ by Giotto di Bondone

Ruins of the Roman Forum

Another Ancient Witness

A Jewish historian named Josephus is another important nonbiblical witness. He was born around A.D. 37 and wrote a twenty-volume history of the Jewish people. In that history he mentioned Jesus and the early Christians. Josephus himself was not a Christian and had no reason to lie about the facts. This is what he wrote about Jesus:

> He was a doer of startling deeds, a teacher of people who received the truth with pleasure. And he gained a following both among many Jews and among many of Greek origin. . . . And when Pilate, because of an accusation made by the leading men among us, condemned him to the cross, those who had loved him previously did not cease to do so. . . . And up until this very day the tribe of Christians, named after him, has not died out.

Antiquities of the Jews, 18

It is clear, then, from the witness of Pliny, Tacitus, Josephus, and other ancient writers as well that Jesus did exist. This fact is accepted by believers and nonbelievers alike. When we talk about Jesus in Scripture, we are talking about someone real. It is not like talking about the gods and goddesses of ancient mythology or other imaginary individuals. Our conclusion must be that the New Testament rests on the very solid fact that Jesus existed and that he made an impact on history. Now it is time for us to turn from the truth we know from the outside to the truth we know from the inside.

This book invites you to look at Jesus Christ in a new way. It will take thought and work. Are you willing to launch out into the deep water? Write your thoughts in your journal.

Scripture INSIGHT

The words of Sacred Scripture and other ancient documents were not written originally on paper. They were written on papyrus, an inexpensive material made from a plant that grew in the marshes along the Nile River in Egypt. Parts of the plant were pressed together. After these were dried and rubbed smooth, they could be written upon. The papyrus was formed into long sheets and rolled around a cylinder, making a scroll. Sometimes smaller pieces of papyrus were cut off the scroll to use for short letters or notes. Typically, however, a long scroll would be used for lengthy documents, such as a book of the Bible or other important works.

Later on, parchment was more widely used for writing. Parchment was a writing material made from animal skin. It was washed and the fur removed; then the skin was treated, stretched on a frame, and rolled into scrolls.

Fragments of ancient scrolls that contain parts of the Bible can be found around the world. Many of them are in the Vatican Library.

The Truth from Inside

A person doesn't need faith to establish the fact that Jesus of Nazareth existed and that he had a profound influence on the history of the world. None of this can be denied. For a person of faith, however, there is so much more to Jesus than a few bare facts from history. What do we as people of faith know about him? Where can we connect with this individual who changed the world and who is at the center of the Christian religion?

Our roots go back to the apostles, who were Jesus' closest friends and followers. They were chosen by him, and for about three years they lived with him and walked with him and listened to all he taught them. What they passed on to the other disciples about these experiences has been faithfully preserved by the Church for all time.

How did the Church community do this? At first it was done through *oral tradition*. This means that what the apostles experienced about Jesus and what they learned from him were passed on by word of mouth. The earliest members of the Church saw no need to write anything down in the form of an official record of Jesus. After all, the Lord Jesus himself left no written document of his life or teaching.

Moreover, like other teachers of his time, Jesus taught by the spoken word. His disciples, like the disciples of all great teachers of that time, remembered his words and discussed them. This was not unusual; the disciples were people of their time. They were not highly educated, nor were they practiced in the art of writing. Like many ancient people, however, they were accustomed to committing words and ideas to memory.

Even after the resurrection there was still no need to write down anything because the apostles and other eyewitnesses to Jesus were still alive. If people wanted to know something about Jesus, all they had to do was talk to these

An apostle giving testimony about Jesus at a public gathering, Raphael, 16th century

eyewitnesses and close friends of the Lord. They could also speak to Mary, his mother. Another reason formal written records were not kept from the start was that the community expected that Jesus would return to them very soon.

More Than Word of Mouth

Oral tradition was not the only way people expressed their faith in Jesus. Whenever the Christian community gathered for liturgy, they sang psalms from the Old Testament as well as other hymns that had been composed about Jesus and what he meant for the world. Many of these hymns were written down, as were creeds and other statements of belief. Early on, people also collected the sayings of Jesus that they had heard from Jesus himself or from the preaching and teaching of the apostles. Nevertheless, these were

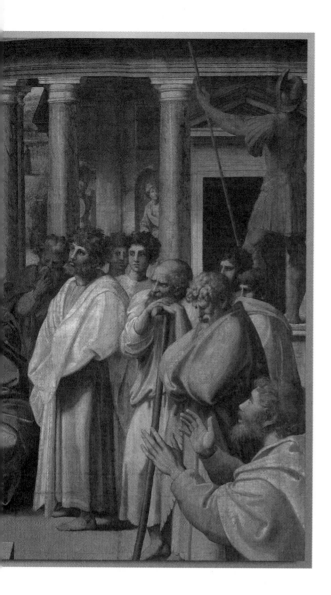

Such good news about the life and teachings of Jesus could not be contained in letters alone. Something more was needed, and the gospel accounts emerged in answer to that need. These gospels began to appear about fifteen years after Paul began to write his letters. Eventually the Church recognized and determined that Paul's letters and four gospel accounts would be part of what we now call the New Testament. These writings came out of the lived experience of the Church and were written under the guidance of the Holy Spirit. They addressed the needs of different Church communities and took shape over a long period of time.

Did the coming of this new testimony about Jesus and his disciples mean that the sacred writings of the Jewish people were no longer needed? No! Nothing could be further from the truth. The early Church revered the writings of the Old Testament and accepted them as the word of God. This "new" testament about Jesus was understood as a completion and fulfillment of what had come before. Far from rejecting the Old Testament, Christians saw even deeper meaning in it.

Imagine that you have the opportunity to talk with Mary, the mother of Jesus. If you could ask her one question about Jesus, what would it be?

private collections and had no official standing or authority in the Church.

It was not long, however, before things changed for the early Church community. People began to realize that the second coming of Jesus was not going to happen immediately, that it would take place at some future time. Then the first apostles began to die. Many feared that soon none of the original followers of Jesus would be left. Where could people turn to make sure that the truth about Jesus and his teaching was being handed on? About twenty years after the death and resurrection of Jesus, what we now describe as the first official writings of the Church began to appear. These were the letters written by Saint Paul to various Christian communities.

CATHOLIC ID

God making himself known to us is called *divine revelation*. Understanding divine revelation is essential to our whole life of faith. In fact it is the basis of everything Christians believe, and it helps to identify who we are as Catholics. God not only revealed himself but made sure that his revelation would be passed on from generation to generation. How did this happen? It happened through the passing on of tradition and the writing of Sacred Scripture. God's revealing activity took place in the history of the community. It also took place over a long period of time and reached its high point in Jesus Christ.

Two Becoming One

To understand Jesus and the Church fully, we must know both the Old and the New Testaments because they belong with each other. That is why we will explore more about both testaments in the next chapter. As we shall see, both the Old and the New Testaments come from God, and both come from the lived experience of God's people. Together the two testaments form one book that we call the Bible, a book unlike any other.

The Bible may look like any other book when it is sitting on the shelf. But nothing could be further from the truth. It is more than a book; it is a library of books. The very word *bible* comes from a word meaning "the books." This describes exactly what the Bible is. It is a collection of seventy-three books that were written over a period of many centuries. Each book was written to hand on a message about faith in God.

The seventy-three books are divided into the Old Testament and the New Testament. The Old Testament is made up of forty-six books. The New Testament is made up of twenty-seven books. All the books together make up the complete Bible.

Take time to look at the chart that gives the names of all seventy-three books of the Bible and how they are divided.

When we use the word *testament*, we are not talking about testifying, or giving witness, as when we speak of a "last will and testament." Rather, *testament* is another word for "covenant." So the Bible is that collection of books that is concerned with God's covenant with us. This was the agreement God made with the people of Israel through Moses (the old covenant). It was brought to fulfillment in Jesus (the new covenant).

Because the Bible is so important in the life of God's people, we generally refer to it as Scripture or Sacred Scripture. The word *scripture* gives us a clue right away that the Bible is the word of God put in writing. As Catholics we know that Scripture cannot stand alone. Scripture and tradition together make present the mystery of Christ in our lives. Scripture and tradition make up "a single sacred deposit" of the word of God (*Catechism*, 97).

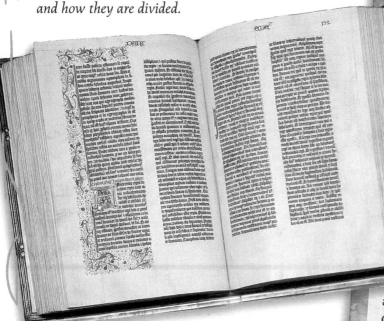

Illuminated pages, Wycliffe Bible, 1440

CATHOLIC TEACHINGS

About the Books of the Bible

After the time of Jesus, the Jewish rabbis who lived in Palestine accepted thirty-nine books as their Scripture. It was written in Hebrew. The early Christians used the Greek translation of the Hebrew Bible. This translation, called the Septuagint, included seven additional books. These were First and Second Maccabees, Tobit, Judith, Sirach, Wisdom, and Baruch. On the basis of apostolic tradition, the Catholic Church officially recognized these forty-six books of the Septuagint as the Old Testament. Today the Jews and most Protestants accept only the thirty-nine books agreed upon in Palestine. That is why Catholic versions of the Bible are different. All Christians, however, accept the same twenty-seven books of the New Testament.

Books of the Bible

The Old Testament

Pentateuch

Genesis   Numbers
Exodus   Deuteronomy
Leviticus

Wisdom Books

Job   Song of Songs
Psalms   Wisdom
Proverbs   Sirach
Ecclesiastes

Historical Books

Joshua   2 Chronicles
Judges   Ezra
Ruth   Nehemiah
1 Samuel   Tobit
2 Samuel   Judith
1 Kings   Esther
2 Kings   1 Maccabees
1 Chronicles   2 Maccabees

Prophetic Books

Isaiah   Obadiah
Jeremiah   Jonah
Lamentations   Micah
Baruch   Nahum
Ezekiel   Habakkuk
Daniel   Zephaniah
Hosea   Haggai
Joel   Zechariah
Amos   Malachi

The New Testament

Gospels

Matthew   Luke
Mark   John

Other Writings

Acts of the   Revelation
Apostles

Letters

Romans   1 Thessalonians   James
1 Corinthians   2 Thessalonians   1 Peter
2 Corinthians   1 Timothy   2 Peter
Galatians   2 Timothy   1 John
Ephesians   Titus   2 John
Philippians   Philemon   3 John
Colossians   Hebrews   Jude

things
to think about

What does it mean for you to know that the words of the New Testament are based on true eyewitness accounts?

Why do you think oral tradition was such an easy and convenient way for ancient peoples to transmit important information and culture?

things
to share

Someone says to you that Jesus is only an imaginary person, that he did not really exist. How would you begin to respond to that statement?

Share with someone the reason why the Old Testament is so important to Catholics.

WORDS TO REMEMBER

Find and define the following:

oral tradition _____
_____
_____

testament _____
_____
_____

OnLine
WITH THE PARISH

Parishes often let people know what the Mass readings will be for the following week. They do this to help people enter more deeply into the celebration of the Eucharist. Try to make it your practice each week to look up the readings in the Bible so that they might become even more alive for you during the Liturgy of the Word. Invite family members to be a part of this experience.

How can ancient, non-Christian documents help us come to an understanding of Jesus?

1

Why is the Bible a book unlike any other book?

2

How many books are there in the Old Testament? Name the four divisions.

3

How many books are there in the New Testament? Name the three divisions.

4

Name and explain one reason why Sacred Scripture is so important for the life of the Church.

5

Life in the Spirit

Many people talk about Scripture but never seem to find time to read it. Make a confidential promise to yourself that during your study of the New Testament, you will read either Matthew's Gospel or Luke's Gospel from beginning to end. To do this, set aside ten minutes each day as your "gospel time." Before reading, you may wish to use this prayer: Lord, be in my heart and on my lips that I may come to love and live the good news each day.

CHAPTER 2

The Divine Word

Be attentive to God's word
"as to a lamp shining in a dark place,
until day dawns and the morning star
rises in your hearts."

2 Peter 1:19

*W*ho wrote the books of the New Testament? of the Old Testament? Who are the authors—or the author—of the Bible? What do you think?

A Question of Authorship

Whenever we write something down, we cannot help but leave clues about ourselves simply by the way we write. Such clues might include a favorite word or phrase, the point of view that we use, a peculiar style of expression, or even the choice of subject. There are also regional expressions that can hint at the identity of a writer. Depending on where one lives in the United States, for example, soft drinks are called either "soda" or "pop." In some areas of the country, a person is described as standing "in line"; in other places, the expression is standing "on line."

It is easy to see that what we say and what we write tell us many things. We can guess at people's educational background, their place of birth and the neighborhood where they grew up, their experiences and the type of work they do, and even the kind of people with whom they have associated. Obviously our guesswork will not tell us everything, but it can provide many pieces to help fit together the puzzle of human identity.

The Bible, too, gives us clues about its authorship. When we move from book to book among the seventy-three books of Sacred Scripture, we detect the hands of different authors at work. We become aware of different expressions and styles of writing, different points of view and reasons for writing. Some books are more exciting and more colorful than others. Some writers, such as the author of

Two pages from the *Codex Sinaiticus,* the oldest complete New Testament known to exist

Luke's Gospel and the Acts of the Apostles, were better storytellers than others. Some came from a background of power and influence, and others came from more humble surroundings. A few of the writers may have been teachers or lawyers. Some of the writers of the Old Testament may have been priests of the Jewish religion. In any event it does not take much time and effort to determine that the Bible is the work of many different authors.

Is the Bible only a collection of various authors' works? Yes and no. As Catholics we believe that the Bible had many authors and, at the same time, that the Bible had only one author. This means two things:

- The many authors of the Bible were its human authors. They were the literary sources of the books. Like the authors of any writings, they themselves chose the words, the expressions, the stories, the names of characters, and all things that go into the making of a written document. No one else did it for them.

- At the same time God is the author of Scripture. This is because all the books of the Bible and all the words in them were written under the influence of the Holy Spirit. This is what we call divine inspiration.

Divine inspiration is the special influence of the Holy Spirit on the human authors of the Bible. Because of this influence, God himself becomes the authority behind Scripture and therefore becomes in the deepest sense its author, too. For this reason we call the Bible the word of God. That is why the sublime message of Scripture surpasses mere human invention.

Inspiration is an extremely important concept in the study and appreciation of Sacred Scripture. If we do not have a clear and well-grounded understanding of inspiration, the true meaning of Scripture—both the Old Testament and the New Testament—will be lost. If we do not have this understanding, the Bible becomes just like any other book sitting on a library shelf.

The Bible, however, is not like any other book. It has a divine origin and authority. This is what the Catholic Church teaches us: "God is the author of Sacred Scripture because he inspired its human authors; he acts in them and by means of them. He thus gives assurance that their writings teach without error his saving truth" (*Catechism,* 136).

Let's explore this wonderful mystery of the Bible's authorship more fully.

What was your first clue that the Bible is more than the product of human hands alone?

A Divine Author

What do most people think of when they hear the word *author*? They probably think of someone using a keyboard or paper and pen to put down his or her thoughts. There are some authors, however, who dictate their words and ideas into a machine or to another person who copies them down.

Is this what we mean when we say that God is the author of the Bible? Did God himself actually write down the words or dictate them to the human authors of the Bible? Not at all. God did not do either one of these things. Many people, however, used to think that God worked in that way. We call this the *dictation theory of inspiration*.

According to the dictation theory, God alone is the author of the Bible. He dictated every single word—and the punctuation, too! The human being who copied down God's words was nothing more than a robot and made no contribution to God's dictation.

This is a simple theory, but it is really too simple. The problem with such a theory is that God would never act in that way. After all, God created human beings in his own image and would never treat them in such a manner. He would want each human author of the Bible to make his own particular contribution to the writing and reflect his own personality. God would never use human beings as if they were unthinking machines.

For all these reasons the Catholic Church rejects the dictation theory of inspiration. The Second Vatican Council taught that God, the divine author, speaks in Sacred Scripture "through men in human fashion" (*Divine Revelation,* 12).

Other Mistaken Notions

The dictation theory, which makes God alone the author of the Bible, is not the only mistake people have made about divine inspiration. Some people have gone to the other extreme. They hold that human beings alone were the authors of the Bible. According to this theory God did not really have much to do with the writing of Scripture except to prevent the human author from falling into error. God provided no new information. We call this idea the *God-as-assistant theory.*

Such a theory reduces Scripture to a mere human enterprise and makes it more like a textbook on faithful living. Then Scripture is no longer God's word; it is not the divine word. Naturally the Church rejects this theory, too.

Another approach to inspiration suggested by some people might be called the *later-approval theory*. According to this idea the Bible was written in the same way as every other book. Then, when the Church accepted the writings as sacred, it was understood that the Holy Spirit was approving them. But the problem with this theory is the idea that the Holy Spirit had nothing to do with the biblical writings before the Church approved them. Like the God-as-assistant theory, this type of thinking makes Scripture a nice book but not the word of God. That is why the Church rejects this theory, too.

These mistaken notions about divine inspiration were thought up in the past. Unfortunately they still have an effect on people's thinking today. People who accept some form of the dictation theory can be described as strict fundamentalists. They take every word of the Bible literally. They accept every word at its face value and never look at the deeper meaning behind it.

Consider, for example, the following saying of Jesus: "It is easier for a camel to pass through the eye of a needle than for one who is rich to enter the kingdom of God" (Matthew 19:24). If we take these words literally, no rich person would have a chance to get to heaven. But that is not what is meant here. These words are obviously an exaggeration for effect. They teach a message in a clear and colorful way that

In the liturgy of the Catholic Church, we often read Sacred Scripture from both the Old Testament and the New Testament. After the first two readings, the lector says, "The word of the Lord." After the gospel is proclaimed, the priest or deacon says, "The gospel of the Lord." In each case we respond, "Thanks be to God" or "Praise to you, Lord Jesus Christ." We acknowledge that God is the author of Sacred Scripture. In practice, then, Catholics profess their belief in divine inspiration at every liturgy.

people can understand, but they should never be taken literally. To take them literally distorts the truth of God's message.

On the other hand, some people hold an opposite view and do not take God's word seriously at all. For these people the words of Scripture carry about as much importance as a book of recipes. This is because for them God really is not the author, if he had anything at all to do with Scripture. Sadly these people often want to interpret Scripture to serve themselves.

The real truth about divine inspiration is more complex but also much more exciting and satisfying. This is because it respects both divine authorship and human authorship.

Why do you think people are tempted to accept mistaken notions about inspiration?

God's Revealing Activity

When Jesus and members of the early Church used the word *Scripture*, they were referring to what we now call the Old Testament. They believed that these sacred writings were divinely inspired, and this belief was handed down to them from their Jewish heritage. Before the time of Christ, belief in biblical inspiration was common in Judaism. So it was a part of Jesus' beliefs and those of the early Church, too.

From the earliest days of the Church, the idea of inspiration was accepted and applied to the writings of the New Testament as well. For almost nineteen centuries belief in divine inspiration remained unquestioned. But in modern times people began to question everything, and different theories about inspiration were developed, some of which we have already seen. It was not until the Second Vatican Council opened in 1962 that the Church considered writing a document giving a clear and detailed teaching about divine inspiration and its importance.

The document produced by the council is called the *Dogmatic Constitution on Divine Revelation*. It deals with God's revelation of himself to us and how that revelation is transmitted through time. God revealed himself and his intentions for us at a particular time in history to a particular group of people. He did this first in the community of Israel and later in the apostolic community of the Church. God's revelation was made known by the testimony of those who received it. Passed on by word of mouth, it became *tradition*. Recorded in writing under the inspiration of the Holy Spirit, it became *Scripture*.

In presenting a clear explanation of inspiration, the Vatican II document indicates the strong New Testament foundation for our belief in divine inspiration. Here are two important passages with which Catholics should be familiar:

- "All scripture is inspired by God" (2 Timothy 3:16).

Old and New Testament figures, detail from painting by Fra Angelico, 14th century

• "There is no prophecy of scripture that is a matter of personal interpretation, for no prophecy ever came through human will; but rather human beings moved by the holy Spirit spoke under the influence of God" (2 Peter 1:20–21).

Understanding Inspiration

A book that has both divine and human authorship is unique in human history. We cannot compare the Bible and its origins with any other book or type of writing. So when we talk about inspiration, we are dealing with a mystery of faith. By calling it a mystery, we do not mean that it is totally beyond our understanding. It simply means that there is much more to inspiration than we will ever fully understand.

That being the case, what can we say about God's activity in inspiring the human authors? In a marvelous way God somehow moved the minds of the human authors. He did this so that they could produce works they otherwise would not have been able to write. For example, the powerful and yet loving portrait of God given to us by Paul in his letters could never have come from Paul alone. Nevertheless, in moving Paul's mind and heart, God respected his freedom. That is why Paul's letters are different from other books of the Bible. The letters are truly the work of Paul and inspired by God, too. Both God and Paul are the authors.

How exactly did the Holy Spirit inspire the human authors? The Holy Spirit guided them in the content of their writing and in choosing the truth God wanted taught. The human authors looked at the traditions of the faith community and the opinions that were held by different members of that community. Under the influence of the Holy Spirit, they made the right choices that would transmit the truth God intended for all people.

When people of faith come to the Bible and enter more deeply into the mystery of inspiration, they come face-to-face with the divine word. The *Catechism* expresses this beautifully: "In Sacred Scripture, the Church constantly finds her nourishment and her strength, for she welcomes it not as a human word, 'but as what it really is, the word of God.' 'In the sacred books, the Father who is in heaven comes lovingly to meet his children, and talks with them'" (104).

 Use one of the Scripture passages in today's lesson as part of your evening prayer.

Scripture INSIGHT

Inspiration is a very colorful term. It comes from a word meaning "to breathe." From Old Testament times the image of breathing was applied to God's influence upon the human authors of the Bible. So it was the "breath of God" that came upon the prophets and gospel writers. Their work had authority in the community because it was filled with the very breath of God. This image of "breath" can help us understand the true meaning of inspiration and why we can say God's word is alive and powerful.

The Real Truth

Does being inspired mean that the Bible cannot contain any errors? The answer is yes if we mean that the Bible does not contain any errors about the truths of faith. But what about the truths of history and science? Before modern times, questions of faith, history, and science were all mixed together without any distinctions. In fact most people felt that the Bible was concerned with more than just questions of faith. They looked to the Bible to answer just about every kind of question, even those dealing with science.

Things began to change in the sixteenth century, during the time of Copernicus. He was a Polish astronomer whose theories about the movement of the Sun challenged the way people looked at their world. Until that time people thought that the whole universe revolved around planet Earth. Earth and humankind formed the center of everything. The evidence for this Earth-centered existence was easy to see. People's everyday experience led them to believe that the Sun revolved around Earth. The Sun "rose" in the east and "set" in the west.

There was more than visual evidence, however. People thought the Bible itself, God's holy word, testified to an Earth-centered world. According to their reading of Scripture, God put the Sun, the Moon, and the stars in the sky for our benefit. Think what happened when Copernicus said that Earth revolved around the Sun. No longer was Earth the center of the universe. Copernicus's theory seemed to mean that we could not trust our experience and that the Bible was in error. If the Bible was wrong about this, could it be wrong in other areas?

Over time it has become clear that the truth of Scripture is the truth of faith, truths for our salvation. The Bible does not teach every kind of truth in the world. It is not our primary source for the truth of history or science, for example. The Church teaches that "the books of Scripture must be acknowledged as teaching firmly, faithfully, and without error that truth which God wanted put into the sacred writings for the sake of our salvation" (*Divine Revelation,* 11).

The Church's Book

Knowing about inspiration helps us to understand how the Church chose the writings that would be part of the Bible. After all, there were many important writings that were held in high esteem and circulated among the various communities of the early Church. Along with the seventy-three books chosen to be in the Bible, there were the beautiful letters of Ignatius of Antioch and those of Clement of Rome, just to name a few. There were even other gospel accounts besides those of Matthew, Mark, Luke, and John. One of the most famous was called the Gospel of Thomas.

From all the writings that were in circulation, the Church, guided by the Holy Spirit, recognized only seventy-three as being truly inspired by God. How did the Church do this? For one thing, it saw in these books a certain sublime quality that other works just did not have. More than this, the books seen as sacred played a special role in the faith life of the Church. They expressed the Church's apostolic tradition and origin. They had a real authority about them. Most important, the Church saw in these books a true and necessary reflection that mirrored its own faith.

Already in apostolic times the books of the Old Testament were accepted as Scripture. By the beginning of the second century, official lists of New Testament books were being developed. In fact, by A.D. 200 a Christian writer named Tertullian was the first to use the term *New Testament*. Christians saw in these books standards of their faith and practice.

The seventy-three books of the Bible are called the canon of Sacred Scripture. The English word *canon* comes from a Greek word meaning "measuring rod." In the Church it came to signify a measuring rod of faith. Catholics use the word when speaking about the official list of biblical books, the *canon of Scripture*.

From all this we can truly see that the Bible is the Church's book. It was the Church that assembled these books. It is the Church that has passed them on through the centuries. It is the Church that interprets them in the light of its own tradition. The Bible comes from the Church and serves the Church. The *Catechism* states this very beautifully: "Sacred Scripture is written principally in the Church's heart rather than in documents and records, for the Church carries in her Tradition the living memorial of God's Word" (113).

The *Catechism* also states that in Scripture "the Father who is in heaven comes lovingly to meet his children, and talk with them" (104). How might these words affect you each time you read or listen to Scripture?

CATHOLIC TEACHINGS

About Inspiration

This is what the Second Vatican Council has to say about inspiration: "Holy Mother Church, relying on the belief of the apostles, holds that the books of both the Old and New Testament in their entirety, with all their parts, are sacred and canonical because, having been written under the inspiration of the Holy Spirit they have God as their author and have been handed on as such to the Church" (*Divine Revelation*, 11).

PUTTING IT TOGETHER

things
to think about

Why is it important to know that God is the author of Sacred Scripture?

What does it mean to you to know that Scripture is written in the "Church's heart"?

things
to share

Someone says that the Bible is just like any other book. How would you respond?

One of your friends believes that everything in the Bible is literally true. What example might you give to show that the Catholic approach to the Bible is not like a fundamentalist's view?

WORDS TO REMEMBER

Find and define the following:

divine inspiration _____

_____

_____

canon of Scripture _____

_____

_____

OnLine
WITH THE PARISH

Many parishes have summer Bible classes for young children to help them learn more about the beautiful stories of Scripture. Find out how your group can help in this parish activity.

1. Explain how the Bible has both one author and many authors.

2. What do we mean by the "dictation theory of inspiration"? What does the Church think of this theory?

3. What do we mean when we say that the Bible is the Church's book?

4. Does the fact that the Bible is an inspired book mean that it cannot contain any errors? Explain.

5. How did the individual books become part of the canon of Scripture?

Life in the Spirit

A lectern is the place from which Scripture is proclaimed in a church. When a new lectern is blessed, we hear the following prayer to God the Father:

> We pray that in this church
> we may listen to the voice of
> your Son,
> so that, responding to the
> inspiration of the Holy Spirit,
> we may not be hearers only
> but doers of your word.
> *Book of Blessings*

Use these words as part of your prayer this week.

CHAPTER 3

More Than History

The light shines in the darkness,
and the darkness has not overcome it.

John 1:5

Jesus used the story of Jonah, one of the best-known characters of the Old Testament, to get a point across to his disciples. According to the story, Jonah was swallowed by a whale and lived in its belly for three days. Would you be surprised if someone told you that this story was not based on historical fact but was told to teach a lesson of faith? Why?

Inspiration and History

Actually there are many people who would be surprised to learn that Jonah and his whale were not historical characters. After all, the Bible is the inspired word of God. They think this means that everything in the Bible must be history and therefore based on facts.

Is this true? Does inspiration make everything history? Of course not. Obviously there are many

historical facts in the Bible, but not everything mentioned in the Bible is history. The Book of Jonah, to which Jesus referred, is a good example. It is not inspired history. Rather, it is an inspired parable, a story used to teach a lesson. In the parable Jonah is commissioned by God to preach to the people of a far-off city. But Jonah is afraid and takes a ship and sails away from his responsibility.

The ship is caught in a storm, and Jonah is thrown overboard and swallowed by a great whale. After three days and nights, the whale spits Jonah out onto the shore, and he sets off to carry out the mission given to him by God.

The story of Jonah teaches many important lessons. One lesson is the truth that God wants people to face their responsibilities and never be afraid of doing God's work. Jesus himself gave another meaning to the story of Jonah. He said, "Just as Jonah was in the belly of the whale three days and three nights, so will the Son of Man be in the heart of the earth three days and three nights" (Matthew 12:40). Jesus used the story of Jonah and the whale to teach about his own death and resurrection. Whether or not Jonah was a historical figure makes no difference to the inspired writing or the truth of these lessons.

There are, however, numerous examples of history in the Bible. In the Old Testament the many stories of King David are based on the truth of a famous king of Israel who lived about three thousand years ago. In the New Testament the missionary journeys of Saint Paul show how the Church undertook the spread of the gospel in the first century. David and Paul were not like Jonah; they were real people. They are part of the history of God's people, not imaginary characters only used to make a point in a parable.

So the Bible has some history in it, but it is more than just a listing of cold, hard facts about people and events. The Bible is an inspired book about religious truth. What does this mean? It means that the human authors of the Bible, under the inspiration of the Holy Spirit, interpreted events and people. The authors looked for deeper meaning behind the things that went on in their lives. They looked for religious truth, the truth that God intended to reveal. In seeking after this truth, the writers were more than reporters simply giving facts about what they observed. For the writers of Scripture, the truth was more than the eye could see or more than meets the eye!

What, then, was the primary concern of the biblical writers? Can we describe it in one word or phrase? Yes, we can: *divine revelation,* which is God making himself known to us. The sacred writers wanted to transmit a written record of that revealing activity of God. That is why historical events and even scientific facts were of secondary importance to them.

The fullness of God's revelation comes to us in Jesus, the Word made flesh. John's Gospel summarizes it this way: "No one has ever seen God. The only Son, God, who is at the Father's side, has revealed him" (John 1:18). Jesus is this only Son. When we go to Scripture to discover more about him, we are not looking at Scripture as we would look at a modern history book. We are looking for religious truth, the deeper meaning that God intends to reveal to us. We are looking to encounter Jesus Christ, the Son of God, the second person of the Blessed Trinity who took on flesh at the incarnation.

 *Can you explain the difference between historical fact and religious truth in the Bible? Share your thoughts with the group.*

People with a History

When we say that the primary interest of the biblical writers was religious truth, we are not trying to say they were not at all interested in the facts of history. What happened in history was certainly important to them, for it was in the events of history that God dealt with his people. It was in history that Abraham was called by God. It was in history that the only Son of God was born into the world. It was in history that Jesus chose his apostles and founded the Church. The bottom line is this: The inspired word of God was written in human history, not outside it.

As we look back into history, we often have questions about the day-to-day lives of our ancestors in faith. We may even wonder about the unknown details of Jesus' life. Did he have a favorite sport that he liked to play? What was his favorite meal? Did he enjoy music? Did he like to sing? Did he have a dog or other pet?

These are the kinds of questions that biographers and historians like to answer when writing about well-known people of history. Answers to questions such as these help to make the "story" of history come alive. Food, music, sports, and pets are part of life. They have a human interest to which people relate very easily.

So, did Jesus have a dog or didn't he? We will never know. That question or detail would never have crossed the minds of the biblical writers. When writing about historical people and real events, their approach was completely different from that of modern biographers and historians.

History and History

Modern people approach the truth of history differently from ancient people. Modern people can read, and books and other written materials are readily available. In the ancient world this was not always the case. Few people could read; there were no corner bookstores or libraries. What did ancient people do? They memorized things and passed them on by word of mouth. That is why ancient writers frequently set facts and events into the form of a story that was easy to remember. This might explain their seeming disinterest in reporting exact facts and specific dates. They were more interested in interpreting an event than in describing it as a reporter would.

An important characteristic of ancient writers was their dependence on oral tradition rather than on written records. Unlike modern writers, they did not depend on research and written documents. Modern writers become very involved in giving specific dates, listing the sequence of events exactly, and being able to document all facts. Ancient writers would not feel at home or comfortable in reporting the news of the day!

Nonetheless, ancient writers transmitted the truth in their own way. Although this way was different from ours, it was still based on the truth of history.

Passing on tradition by word of mouth

34

One of the many modern means of communication

The inspired writers of the Bible were no different from other ancient writers. They, too, took the events of their history and wrote about them as other people of their time did. They felt free to interpret their history and discover its meaning. They had wonderful memories, told exciting stories, and depended primarily on oral tradition for the passing on of information in the community of faith.

This is clear when we look at the formation of the gospels in the New Testament. This process took place in three stages.

- Stage 1: *The life and teachings of Jesus.* Jesus actually lived and moved among us in history. The gospel accounts are based on the ministry of Jesus, what he did and taught from about the years A.D. 28 to 30.
- Stage 2: *The oral tradition.* The followers of Jesus spread the good news about him. The apostolic preaching, in which the early Church interpreted the meaning of what Jesus said and did, lasted until about the year A.D. 65. By this date many of the apostles may have died.

- Stage 3: *The written gospels.* Finally the gospel writers selected what was important from oral tradition and put it into written form. They did this under the inspiration of the Holy Spirit. This happened in the first century A.D. between the late 60s and the early 90s.

Now we know the difference between ancient and modern writings about history. That is why we can say there is history, and there is history.

 Are you disappointed about not knowing whether or not Jesus had a dog? Why or why not?

CATHOLIC ID

Saint Thérèse of Lisieux is one of the Church's most popular saints. In her autobiography she spoke about her love of Sacred Scripture: "Above all it's the gospels that occupy my mind when I'm at prayer." Why would she say this? Because the gospels are "the heart of all the Scriptures" (*Catechism*, 125). The gospels are our chief source for the life and teaching of Jesus, our Savior.

Prose and Poetry

The written word can be a powerful thing. It can make people fall down with laughter, or it can bring people to tears. It can transmit such important information that it will move people to change their lives. Nowhere is this more true than in the Bible. This written word of God has been changing people's lives for centuries. The biblical writings, however, are from the past. Do writers from the past share anything in common with modern-day writers?

All writers, whether ancient or modern, have to answer the same question: "What form will my writing take?" Every piece of literature—and this includes the Bible—has its own appropriate literary form. A *literary form* is the type of writing that an author uses to get a message across. The two most basic literary forms are prose and poetry. This book, for example, is written in prose. Why? Because *prose* is the literary form closest to our spoken language, and this makes it more appropriate for study. We use prose when we want to make direct statements about something or to present facts. We also use it to give a running narration in a story.

Poetry, on the other hand, is a different type of literary form. It expresses the truth in another way. *Poetry* is not like our everyday language; it is a more imaginative type of writing that uses symbols, sounds, and rhythms that express things about our life in a more emotional way. We use poetry to describe experiences that the language of prose really cannot express. Consider, for example, the figurative images in the following lines:

> If I could walk in the meadow of sky
> with the sickle moon in my hand,
> I'd cut all the blossoming point-petaled flowers
> 'til knee-deep in stars I'd stand.

What a beautiful picture these words give us. When we look up into the starry sky, it is almost as if we could be knee-deep in stars. Could this ever be expressed more powerfully by using prose? It could not. Poetry is the better literary form in this case. Sometimes poetry can get us into the deeper meaning of things. That is why the words of a song are often in poetic form.

Awareness of literary forms is important in understanding literature. There is a big difference in the way one reads prose and poetry. This awareness is important when we read the Bible, for the Bible is literature, too. It contains the literary forms of prose and poetry. Knowing this will help us to unlock the meaning of this ancient text. In doing so, it will release the power of this divine and human word for modern people.

If I could walk in the meadow of sky
with the sickle moon in my hand,
I'd cut all the blossoming point-petaled flowers
'til knee-deep in stars I'd stand.

Gospel: A Literary Form

The Old Testament and the New Testament have many other literary forms. In this text, however, we will be concentrating on the literary forms that are characteristic of the New Testament. The first and most recognizable literary form is the gospel.

A *gospel* is an announcement of good news. In fact, the word itself means "good tidings." In the New Testament there are four gospels: the Gospels of Matthew, Mark, Luke, and John. Each one announces the good news of salvation in Jesus Christ. It does this not simply to tell the story of Jesus but also to proclaim in faith what Jesus, the Son of God, did for the world. The inspired words of the gospel are not only meant to share the message of Jesus. They are also meant to move those who hear the message to make a commitment to change their lives. That is why Paul could write, "Conduct yourselves in a way worthy of the gospel of Christ, so that, whether I come and see you or am absent, I may hear news of you, that you are standing firm in one spirit, with one mind struggling together for the faith of the gospel" (Philippians 1:27).

More than any other New Testament book, the gospels give the story of Jesus and the most important events of his life. Although there is much biographical detail in the gospels, their primary purpose is not to present a biography of Jesus. Rather they hand on the high point of God's revelation to us in Jesus Christ. That is why they prompt us to change our lives. There is really only one gospel, only one "good news" about Jesus. The four gospel accounts of Matthew, Mark, Luke, and John come to us from different early Christian communities. Their lives as followers of Jesus helped to shape the writing of these gospel proclamations.

 Which do you like to read most, prose or poetry? Explain.

Catholic Teachings

About Bible Translations

The Bible is always being translated from Latin, Greek, and Hebrew into modern languages. In this way people around the world have access to God's word. The Church is very careful that these translations be as correct as possible. That is why all authorized Catholic versions of the Bible must contain an imprimatur. *Imprimatur* is a Latin word meaning "let it be printed." The imprimatur is an approval given by a bishop to print a book. It assures us that a specific translation of the Bible is faithful to the word of God and is the result of good scholarship. Look for the imprimatur statement in the Bible you are using. It can usually be found in the first few pages of the book.

More Literary Forms

Besides prose, poetry, and gospel, there are other literary forms in the New Testament. Here are some that you may easily recognize.

Epistle   The word *epistle* means "letter." In the New Testament there are twenty-one epistles of varying lengths and by different authors. The most famous epistle writer was Saint Paul. Most of his letters were written to Church communities. Some letters, however, were written to individuals who had important responsibilities in the community.

Parable   Parable comes from a word that means "to compare." A *parable* is a fictitious (made-up) short story that uses ordinary experiences of life to teach a deeper spiritual lesson. In a wonderful way parables shake us up and make us see and compare things about life in a whole new way. By twists and turns they challenge us and make us ask questions about our lives.

Think of the parables of the sower and the seed (Matthew 13:1–9), the prodigal son (Luke 15:11–32), and the Good Samaritan (Luke 10:29–37). After reading these passages, we can see why Jesus was such a master teller of parables.

Hymn   The members of the early Church, like those of today's Church, sang hymns and songs when they gathered for the liturgy and other celebrations. This music expressed some of their deepest beliefs. Some of the words from these hymns were incorporated into the New Testament text. One of the most beautiful hymns summarized belief in the humanity and divinity of Jesus. It must have been very popular because Paul made it part of his letter to the Philippians (2:5–11).

Genealogy   A *genealogy* is a listing of ancestors. This listing might be done for a person, a family, or a group. It helps us to know where we come from. The most famous New Testament genealogy is in Matthew 1:1–17. In a masterful way it roots Jesus in the history of Israel and in the family of Abraham. When we know who all the people in the genealogy are, we begin to appreciate how God's promises to us are fulfilled in many and varied ways.

Midrash   This is a distinctly Jewish literary form. It was popular with rabbis, who reinterpreted the Old Testament texts for the people of their day. *Midrash* is a style of writing that the New Testament authors used to apply Old Testament accounts to people in the New Testament. Like the rabbis, the gospel writers did this to help make the Old Testament texts meaningful for Christians.

An example of midrash is found in Matthew 2:16–23. In this passage the gospel writer reminds his readers of incidents from the Old Testament. In telling the story of the return of Jesus, Mary, and Joseph from Egypt, Matthew quotes Jeremiah 31:15–17. This Old Testament passage refers to the return of the Israelites from their exile in Babylonia. By his reinterpretation of Jeremiah, Matthew shows that Jesus relived the experiences of the Jewish people.

Apocalyptic Writing   This literary form is highly symbolic and often uses images describing future times and the end of the world. In attempting to describe the last moments of world history, it speaks of catastrophes and a struggle in which God finally destroys the forces of evil. One clear example of this type of writing is found in Matthew 24:29–31. In this passage we read about the sun being darkened, the moon not giving light, the stars falling from the sky, and even the sound of trumpets announcing the

end of everything. Obviously this type of writing is very symbolic and is not meant to be taken literally.

Is it easy to find all these literary forms in the books of the New Testament? Yes and no. It is easy to spot some of them, especially when we read the text carefully. But we have to be aware that they can be mixed together even in the same chapter of a book. As we shall see, the gospel writers can move very quickly from prose to poetry, from genealogy to midrash to parable. That is why Catholics depend on the guidance of the Church and the insight of Scripture scholars to identify these literary forms.

Why did the biblical writers use so many forms? Because they were dealing with the truth of divine mysteries. One form is not sufficient to express this kind of truth. Poetry gets to the truth in a way different from that of prose. Parables give us the truth in ways different from apocalyptic writings. Yet, the goal of each literary form is the same: to get at the truth. And the truth is larger than any single literary form can contain. Certainly now we can see that the New Testament is much more than history.

 Find the hymn in Philippians 2:5–11. Now pray it together.

things to think about

Someone tells you that we should take every word of the Bible literally because God inspired every word of Scripture. Would you agree or disagree? Explain.

The primary concern of the biblical writers is revelation. What does this mean to you?

things to share

Someone says to you that the Bible must be untrue because it has stories that are preposterous, such as the story of Jonah and the whale. What would you say?

Is the gospel "good tidings" for you? In what ways?

WORDS TO REMEMBER

Find and define the following:

midrash _____

_____

_____

apocalyptic writing _____

_____

_____

OnLine WITH THE PARISH

If you and your group were going to write a book about your parish, including both its history and its life, what types of literary forms do you think you would use? Brainstorm as a group, and explain your choices.

1. Explain the following statement: The Bible is an inspired book about religious truth.

2. What do we mean by the term *literary form*?

3. Explain some differences between ancient and modern writing.

4. What are the three stages in the formation of the gospels?

5. Is it easy to spot all the literary forms in the New Testament? Why or why not?

Life in the Spirit

Jesus often used the image of light in his teaching. He said that he was the light of the world and that darkness would never overcome the light. What kind of light has your study of Scripture brought into your life? Pray to the Holy Spirit that you may have deeper understanding of God's word and that you may help others to overcome darkness in their lives.

CHAPTER 4

Jesus and His People

Blessed be the Lord,
the God of Israel,
for he has visited and
brought redemption to his people.

Luke 1:68

A passport gives us basic information, including place of birth and nationality. A passport also contains a recent photo to help identify the person. If Jesus were to have a passport, what information about him would we find on it? What would he look like?

The Son of David

Most people are already aware of the basic information about Jesus. He was born in the town of Bethlehem in the province of Judaea, which was located in the country of Israel. Jesus was a Jew. That was his nationality.

As for his looks, no one can say for sure. But this has not stopped artists through the centuries from painting his image. As men and women of faith, these artists wanted people to recognize in Jesus something of themselves and their own culture. So they painted Jesus to look like the people of their own countries. That is why we have many different images of Jesus today. At times he looks Italian; sometimes he is pictured as Dutch or African or Asian.

Jesus, however, was not Dutch or African or Italian or Asian. Jesus was a Jew who lived about two thousand years ago in a world very different from our own. As a Middle Eastern person of that time, he probably had dark brown eyes, dark hair, and olive-colored skin. These are characteristics of the Semitic peoples who inhabited this region.

We also know that Jesus grew up in the small town of Nazareth in Galilee and more than likely lived the life of a country person. Like his foster father, Joseph, he was known as a carpenter and was accustomed to working with his hands. Jesus knew what it meant to work hard and the effort that it took to build something. Contrary to many pictures that present him as someone who never got his hands dirty, Jesus was probably a rugged individual with calloused hands and muscles toughened from work.

Because Jesus was a Jew, he belonged to a people with a rich history and religious heritage. If we want to know Jesus and make sense of the New Testament, we must know and understand the people whose heritage Jesus shared. Who were his ancestors? When did their history begin?

God formed a people of his own beginning with Abraham. He promised that Abraham's descendants would be "as countless as the stars of the sky and the sands of the seashore" (Genesis 22:17). The God who called Abraham would be their God, and they would be his people. God kept this promise with Abraham and with Isaac, Abraham's son. God continued to keep his promise with Jacob, the son of Isaac, and with Jacob's twelve sons. Their names would later be identified with the twelve tribes of Israel. These twelve tribes, as listed in Genesis 49:1–27, are Reuben, Simeon, Levi, Judah, Zebulun, Issachar, Dan, Gad, Asher, Naphtali, Joseph, and Benjamin. It is important to know their names because they are mentioned in the New Testament, too.

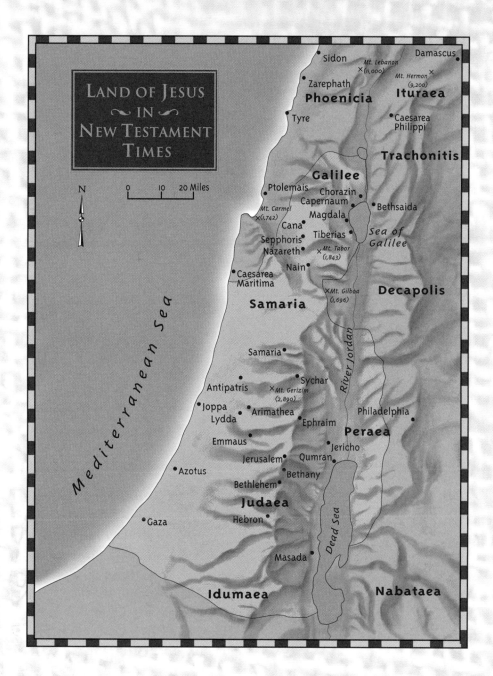

The history of the Jewish people was filled with struggle and hardship as they tried to be faithful to God. We remember that Jesus' ancestors were enslaved in Egypt. Under the leadership of Moses, God led his people to freedom and to the promised land. Guided by judges such as Deborah and Samson, the people conquered and settled this land. God finally gave them kings to rule them, the greatest of whom was King David, a member of the tribe of Judah. Now the Jews would be like other nations, with a king of their own. They would have a great capital, the city of Jerusalem. There David's son Solomon built a magnificent Temple where God could be worshiped.

Later, however, the people forgot God's promise and became careless. They rejected the warnings of the prophets. They turned away from God and were led far away from their homeland into captivity in Babylonia. After many years God, who is always faithful, brought them back to their own land. There the people rebuilt the Temple, which had been destroyed, and they rededicated themselves to the Lord. God, however, was now calling them to be more than a great nation. He was preparing them for the greatest moment in history: the coming of the promised Messiah, the Son of David.

People of the Covenant

Jesus and his disciples were people of their time and used the language of the Jewish religion and culture. Many of the words they used took their meanings from ancient times and came from the Old Testament. If we want to get closer to Jesus and appreciate the New Testament, we have to make these words our own.

One of the most important of these words is *covenant*. People who think they know what a covenant is may be surprised to discover how rich in meaning this word really is.

Political Covenants Originally *covenant* was a political word. A *political covenant* was a treaty made between nations or individuals. Often it was made between a victorious king and the conquered people of another nation. So important was the covenant that it was usually sealed with a religious ceremony or solemn ritual action.

Political covenants were common among the pagan peoples of ancient times. Normally these covenants took a standard form and contained several parts:

- a preface naming the parties of the agreement: the powerful king and the conquered people
- a historical introduction listing the good things the king had done for the people
- the terms of the agreement: the duties and obligations that the conquered people would undertake at the king's direction
- proclamation of the terms to all the people
- witness of pagan gods
- the curses and blessings that would be given by the gods to those who either broke or kept the covenant.

Every treaty was completed with a ceremony. It might be the offering of a sacrifice to the gods, but often it was a ritual action. First an animal was cut in two. Then a representative from each side of the treaty would walk through the middle of the divided animal. This showed that the people who made the treaty understood that the gods might destroy in the same way those who failed to live up to the agreement.

Biblical Covenants When the ancient Israelites wanted to describe their relationship with the one true God, they adopted this covenant format and gave it a religious meaning. A *biblical covenant* was a solemn agreement between God and his people, legally binding on both sides and confirmed by offering a sacrifice to God or by a solemn ritual. The form of this biblical covenant looked very much like that of the ancient political covenant.

In the Old Testament the greatest covenant God made with his people was the covenant on Mount Sinai (Exodus 20—24). This covenant, like an ancient political covenant, also had several parts:

- a preface: "I, the LORD, am your God, who brought you out of the land of Egypt." (Exodus 20:2)
- a historical introduction: a reminder of everything God had done for his people
- terms of agreement: the commandments and laws given to Moses by God
- proclamation by Moses of the terms to all the people

- witness of the one and only God
- curses and blessings: God's promised rewards for the good and punishment for the evil.

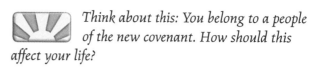

Think about this: You belong to a people of the new covenant. How should this affect your life?

After the people agreed to the terms of the Sinai covenant, it was sealed with a sacrifice. Then they participated in the sacrificial meal. As Moses sprinkled the blood of the sacrifice on the people, he said, "This is the blood of the covenant which the LORD has made with you" (Exodus 24:8). Now God and the people were united. They became one "blood," one family.

Scripture INSIGHT

The people of the Old Testament and of Jesus' time as well were agricultural people, people of the land. When they offered sacrifices to God, they often used animals. They did this, not because they hated animals or wanted to abuse them, but because they wanted to give God the most important things they owned.

Why should we be so concerned with these ancient covenants? Because they are at the heart of both the Old and the New Testaments. Beginning with Noah and continuing with Abraham, Moses, and David, God established a relationship with his people through covenants. God was always faithful to his promises; yet the people needed to be called again and again to renew their promises to God. Eventually the prophets began to speak of a new covenant. This prophecy was fulfilled in Jesus.

Look again at the words of Moses when he sprinkled the people with the blood of the covenant. Do his words remind you of any words in the New Testament? Remember what Jesus said at the Last Supper: "This cup is the new covenant in my blood, which will be shed for you" (Luke 22:20). Jesus was using covenant terminology. He did this for a good reason. Like the covenant at Sinai, this covenant would be sealed in blood—the Blood of Jesus— and a sacrificial meal. Now there was a new covenant between God and his people. It was not sealed with the blood of animals but was ratified once and for all in the Blood of Jesus, the Son of God. This is the new and everlasting covenant in which we share as followers of Christ.

People of the Temple

The Temple in Jerusalem was a very important place for Jesus and the Jews. The gospels record that Jesus was brought there as an infant and again as a twelve-year-old boy on pilgrimage with his family. During his public life Jesus went to the Temple on important occasions. You might remember the time when he got angry with the money changers and drove them away from the Temple area. Why was the Temple so important? What did it have to do with the Jewish people and their faith in God?

The Temple was the center of Jewish life and worship. It was only at the Temple that sacrifices could be offered to God. The offering of sacrifices was an important part of the covenant and of Jewish worship. Every day there were special morning and evening sacrifices offered to the praise of God. A *sacrifice* was a gift offered to God by a priest and destroyed in some way to show that it belonged to God alone.

The different kinds of sacrifices offered in the Temple are listed in the first seven chapters of the Book of Leviticus. The gifts to be sacrificed were brought to the priests. Possible gifts included cattle, sheep, and goats. The poor, such as Mary and Joseph, could offer pigeons or turtledoves. Other sacrificial gifts included grain, flour, frankincense, oil, and bread.

Why were these gifts offered? They were offered to give praise and thanksgiving to God and as a way of atoning for sin. Perhaps the most important sacrifice was the holocaust offering. A *holocaust* was the offering of a whole animal. The person offering the gift would present it to the priest. After the animal was slaughtered, its blood was sprinkled over the altar. Then the offering was totally consumed by fire. Why? To return to God the gift of life that only God could have given in the first place. In the making of this sacrifice, the smoke from the victim went directly up to God. The victim's blood was poured on the altar because blood was considered the force of life itself. Now the gift belonged to God in a special way.

Priesthood and Sacrifice

A *priest* is one authorized to offer a sacrifice. Sacrifice is the highest form of worship one can offer to God, and every sacrifice in the Temple was offered by a priest. In Israel priests were not ordained for sacred service in the way that priests of the new covenant, Catholic priests, are ordained today. The Old Testament priesthood was hereditary, passed on from father to son. God had chosen the tribe of Levi as the priestly class, and a man was a priest simply because he was a member of this tribe.

Model of the Temple rebuilt by Herod around 20 B.C.

During his trial Jesus was brought before the high priest. Try to find the priest's name in the New Testament. Clue: Read John 18.

Priesthood and sacrifice were important for Israel. In fact the entire Book of Leviticus is filled with procedures and regulations about Temple worship and the priesthood. However, when the Temple of Jerusalem was destroyed by the Romans in A.D. 70, the priesthood of the old covenant came to an end. In the new covenant there would be a new priesthood, one centered in Jesus.

In the New Testament we learn that Jesus was both the sacrificial victim and the priest. He gave up his life on the altar of the cross, and through his Blood we were saved from sin. In the Letter to the Hebrews, Jesus Christ is also called our high priest. There we read:

Every high priest is taken from among men and made their representative before God, to offer gifts and sacrifices for sins. . . . No one takes this honor upon himself but only when called by God, just as Aaron was. In the same way, it was not Christ who glorified himself in becoming high priest, but rather the one who said to him:
   "You are my son;
      this day I have begotten you."
Hebrews 5:1–5

Moses and Aaron, his brother, were members of the tribe of Levi. Over the long history of the Jewish people, the family of Aaron was singled out by God as the family from which the Temple priests would come. The other members of the tribe of Levi became secondary ministers of the Temple who assisted the priests. These secondary ministers became known as *Levites*. Do you remember the priest and the Levite who are mentioned in Jesus' parable of the Good Samaritan? Now you know who they are.

With so many members of the tribe of Levi—both priests and Levites—involved in Temple worship, some sort of organization was necessary. The head priest, who exercised overall authority in the Temple, was called the *high priest*. One of his special duties each year was to enter the holy of holies, the most sacred part of the Temple. The high priest alone could do this once a year on the Day of Atonement.

CATHOLIC ID A beautiful part of the ordination ceremony for Catholic priests is the anointing with oil called sacred chrism. Although the priesthood of the Old Testament was hereditary, those priests, too, were anointed with oil as a sign that they were set apart for special service. In Leviticus 8:12, for example, Moses anoints Aaron, his brother.

People of Prayer

An important belief of Jesus and the Jews was that God was present in his people, in the Temple, and in God's law. That was the point of the covenant and its fulfillment: The Jews were God's people, and the Lord of heaven and earth was their God.

God, Present in His People   As a covenant people the Jews were to imitate God. Moses had been instructed by God to tell the people, "Be holy, for I, the LORD, your God, am holy" (Leviticus 19:2). That is why Jesus and his people were to be people of prayer. Every morning and every evening, they recited the great Shema. *Shema* is a word meaning "hear," and it was the first word of the prayer:

Orthodox Jew playing the shofar (ram's horn) to announce the beginning of a Jewish festival

> HEAR, O ISRAEL! THE LORD IS OUR GOD, THE LORD ALONE! THEREFORE, YOU SHALL LOVE THE LORD, YOUR GOD, WITH ALL YOUR HEART, AND WITH ALL YOUR SOUL, AND WITH ALL YOUR STRENGTH.
> DEUTERONOMY 6:4–5

The words of the Shema tell us that because there is only one God, we must love him with our whole being. Jesus recited the words of the Shema every day. He also made them "the greatest and the first commandment" (Matthew 22: 38).

Besides praying the Shema each day, Jesus went to the synagogue in Nazareth. There was only one Temple, and that was in Jerusalem. But every village and town had a *synagogue*. It was a place of prayer and study; the scrolls containing Sacred Scripture were kept there.

Daily services were held in the synagogue, but the main gathering of the week was on the Sabbath. The Sabbath service opened with the singing of a psalm and the recitation of the Shema and other prayers. These were followed by the reading of Scripture and a sermon. The service closed with the blessing prayer found in Numbers 6:24–26.

The *Sabbath observance* was an important part of the covenant between God and his people. It was based on the creation story of Genesis, in which God rested on the seventh day after creating the world. Observing the Sabbath was a serious obligation as part of God's law and was a sign of recognizing God's presence with his people. The Sabbath began at sunset on Friday and lasted until sunset on Saturday. Today, we believe that a new day begins at midnight; but at the time of Jesus, a new day was considered to begin at sunset. No work of any kind could be done on the Sabbath, including housework and cooking a meal.

God, Present in the Temple The Temple was the center of the Jewish religion. It was a sacred place and contained the holy of holies. This was God's special dwelling place with his people, for it was there that the ark of the covenant had been kept. Jews living outside Jerusalem made pilgrimages to the Temple. On the great feasts as many as 200,000 made a pilgrimage to Jerusalem, more than doubling the resident population of 150,000. Three feasts were special times of pilgrimage:

- *Passover,* or Pesah, was a feast for remembering that God brought his people out of slavery in Egypt. It was celebrated in the spring. The passover, or paschal, lambs were sacrificed at the Temple, and the families who were there participated in the sacrificial meal.
- *Pentecost,* or the feast of Weeks, was fifty days after Passover. It celebrated the covenant on Mount Sinai and was a time for renewing the covenant. It was like the anniversary of the giving of God's law to Moses.
- *Tabernacles,* or Sukkoth, was the harvest feast celebrated in autumn. It was a special time to thank God for bringing his people out of Egypt and returning them to the promised land.

In the autumn calendar the *Day of Atonement,* or Yom Kippur, was also an important feast. It was a day of fasting and repentance for sin. On this feast the high priest took two goats as sin offerings. He offered the sacrificial blood of one goat as an offering for sin in the holy of holies, which he alone could enter on this one day each year. He laid his hands upon the head of the other goat and then drove the animal out into the desert. This signified that the sins of Israel would be taken away. The goat that

symbolically carried away the sins of the people was known as a *scapegoat.*

God, Present in His Law
For the Jews the law of God flowed from the covenant, and the obligation to keep it was a covenant duty. God's will for the people took the form of law. Unlike other peoples, for whom all laws were human inventions, Jesus and the other Jews understood God's law as his revealed will. So knowing and living God's law was a privilege and part of a sacred covenant. This meant that God's law was liberating; obeying it was to be a joy!

One of the psalms Jesus prayed was Psalm 119, a prayer to God, the lawgiver. With 176 verses, it is the longest psalm. But all the verses give the same message: May God be praised and thanked for giving us his law; may we have the wisdom to understand it and the strength to keep it.

 Is obeying God's law a joy for you? Try to include part of Psalm 119 in your prayer this week.

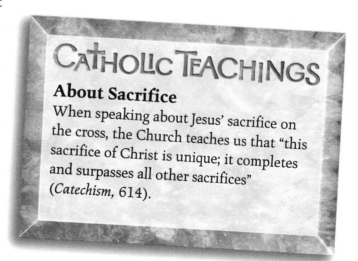

CATHOLIC TEACHINGS
About Sacrifice
When speaking about Jesus' sacrifice on the cross, the Church teaches us that "this sacrifice of Christ is unique; it completes and surpasses all other sacrifices" (*Catechism*, 614).

PUTTING IT TOGETHER

things to think about

Why do you think it is so important for Catholics to remember that Jesus was a Jew?

After studying about Jesus and his people, how do you picture Jesus now? Has your image of him changed? How?

things to share

Someone says to you that Jews and Christians have nothing in common. How would you respond?

Share with someone the reasons why the ideas of sacrifice and priesthood are so important in both the Old Testament and the New Testament.

WORDS TO REMEMBER

Find and define the following:

biblical covenant _____

_____

_____

sacrifice _____

_____

_____

OnLine WITH THE PARISH

Look around your parish church to find images of Jesus in statues, paintings, or stained glass. What image of Jesus do you think the artist or artists tried to portray in their works? What suggestions would you give to an artist about images of Jesus if you were going to design a parish church?

Give one example of the way Jesus and his disciples were people of their time.

1

How did political covenants influence biblical covenants?

2

What did Jesus mean when he said at the Last Supper, "This cup is the new covenant in my blood, which will be shed for you" (Luke 22:20)?

3

Why was the Temple in Jerusalem so important for Jesus and the Jews?

4

Describe one of the Jewish prayer practices used at the time of Jesus.

5

Life in the Spirit

Pray this Good Friday prayer:

Let us pray
for the Jewish people,
the first to hear the word of God,
that they may continue to grow
   in the love of his name
and in faithfulness to his covenant.

Almighty and eternal God,
long ago you gave your promise
   to Abraham and his posterity.

Listen to your Church as we pray
that the people you first made
   your own
may arrive at the fullness of
   redemption.

We ask this through Christ
   our Lord. Amen.

CHAPTER 5

Jesus and His World

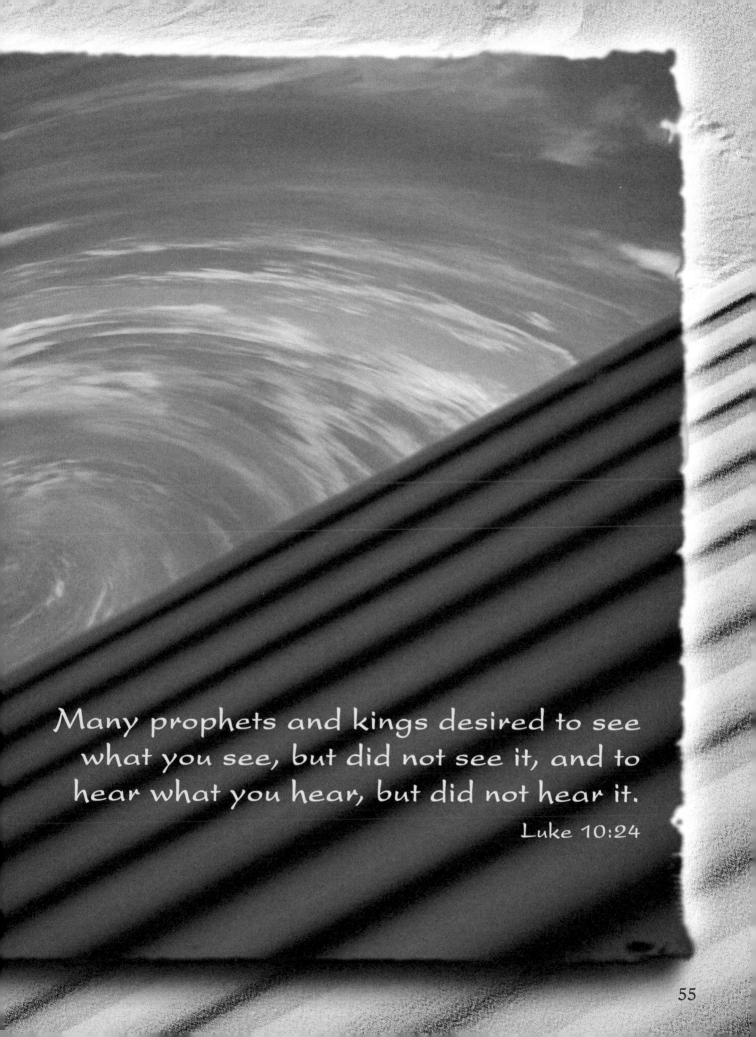

Many prophets and kings desired to see what you see, but did not see it, and to hear what you hear, but did not hear it.

Luke 10:24

A large part of our planet is covered by deserts. Have you ever visited a desert region or seen one on television or in movies? What do you think it would be like to live in a desert?

Crossroads of the World

Jesus grew up and lived in one of the great desert regions of the world. His country, on the edge of a great desert, was called Israel. Later it was called Palestine. Centuries before Jesus the country had been called Canaan and was the land promised by God to Abraham and his descendants.

Israel was a small country, but it had a rich and varied landscape. To the west, it bordered on the Mediterranean Sea. East of the coastal plain was the hill country. This was an area with hills and valleys, excellent for herding sheep and goats and for growing fruits and vegetables. Farther east was a mountain range with high bluffs that descended to the Jordan River valley and finally led to the Arabian Desert.

Because Israel was close to the desert, it is important for readers of the New Testament to understand just what a desert is. The word *desert* covers a variety of landscapes, from shifting sand dunes to rocky cliffs to a hardened mixture of sand and pebbles. Travel in the desert is difficult, even for some animals. Besides the overwhelming heat, the desert is dry and barren, and water wells are found only occasionally on oases.

In an arid country surrounded by so much desert, the Jordan valley was an important place, for it was there that the Jordan River flowed. There, too, was the Sea of Galilee, a beautiful freshwater lake. But the valley also contained the Dead Sea, a salty and lifeless body of water about thirteen hundred feet below sea level (the lowest point on the surface of the earth).

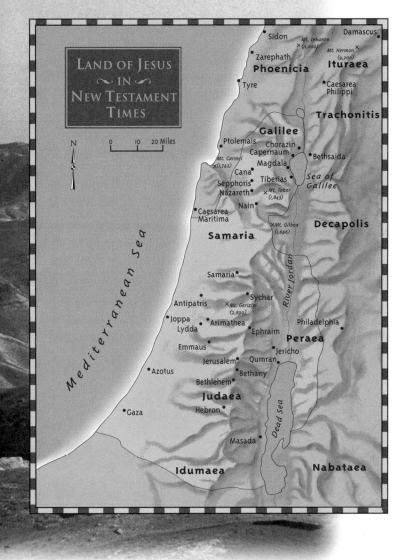

LAND OF JESUS IN NEW TESTAMENT TIMES

N   0   10   20 Miles

Damascus
Sidon
Mt. Lebanon ×(11,000)
Zarephath
Mt. Hermon ×(9,200)
Phoenicia
Ituraea
Tyre
•Caesarea Philippi
Trachonitis
Galilee
Ptolemais•
Chorazin
Capernaum•   •Bethsaida
Magdala
Mt. Carmel ×(1,742)
Cana•
Tiberias
Sea of Galilee
Sepphoris•
Nazareth• ×Mt. Tabor (1,843)
Nain•
Caesarea Maritima•
×Mt. Gilboa (1,696)
Decapolis
Samaria
Samaria•
•Sychar
×Mt. Gerizim (2,890)
Antipatris•
Joppa•   •Arimathea
Lydda•
•Philadelphia
Ephraim•
Peraea
Emmaus•
•Jericho
Jerusalem•   Qumran•
River Jordan
•Azotus
•Bethany
Bethlehem•
Judaea
•Gaza
Hebron•
Masada•
Dead Sea
Idumaea
Nabataea

Mediterranean Sea

emperor in Rome. Supported by a vast army, the governors were to keep order throughout the empire. The day-to-day running of governments was left to the local rulers and kings. But the Roman governors retained overall control. They saw to it that taxes were levied for Rome, and they had the last word in all disputes.

Among all the provinces of the mighty empire, the tiny province of Israel had special privileges. The Jews hated the presence of the pagan Romans in their country and fiercely opposed them. To keep peace, the Romans allowed the Jews to worship their God publicly and did not force them to worship the gods of Rome. In addition the Jews were not subject to military service, could keep the Sabbath, and were allowed to pay a special tax for the upkeep of the Temple.

At the time of Jesus, Israel was made up of three main regions: Galilee, Samaria, and Judaea. Galilee in the north gave its name to the Sea of Galilee. Nazareth was in Galilee, and Jesus was known both as a Nazorean and as a Galilean. Samaria was the middle region in Israel and was populated by a mixed race of people. The Samaritans were descendants of Jews who centuries before had intermarried with pagans. For that reason they were looked down upon by the other Jews of Jesus' time.

Even though Israel could be a harsh land in which to live, it was still known as a crossroads for peoples of the ancient world. A narrow strip of territory along the seacoast, it formed a natural highway for merchants going between the great centers of Mesopotamia and Egypt. But this also made it a highway for the invading armies of ancient empires. Israel, being so small, was often conquered and ruled by one of these foreign powers. At the time of Christ, Israel was part of the Roman Empire.

The Romans are mentioned often in the New Testament. They ruled a mighty empire that stretched from Britain to Egypt. The empire was divided into provinces, each one overseen by a governor or administrator appointed by the

Judaea was south of Samaria and was the center for Jewish worship. No matter where they lived, Jews looked to Judaea, for Jerusalem and its Temple were there. It was the political capital and the seat of religious authority. Jesus was born in Judaea in the town of Bethlehem. In the desert region of Judaea, John the Baptist lived and preached. It was in the district of Judaea that Jesus carried on much of his ministry and was crucified. So Israel was more than at a crossroads of the world; it was at the crossroads of faith.

How do you think a knowledge of Israel will help you to understand Jesus and his message in a deeper way?

57

A View from Nazareth

Knowing more about Galilee helps us to know more about Jesus. The upper part of this region was very mountainous and sparsely populated. It was a place where someone could get away from the busyness of life and enjoy the solitude of the countryside. The lower part of Galilee, however, was a heavily populated area that included both Gentiles and Jews. It was the place where Jesus grew up. One reason for the larger population in this area was its closeness to the Sea of Galilee and the big fishing industry there. In fact, fish that swam in these waters were caught and then sold throughout the Roman Empire.

Nazareth, the town where Jesus spent most of his life, was in lower Galilee. The Jews who lived there were exposed to many outside influences. Perched on a hillside, Nazareth looked down on a major trading route called the *Via Maris* ("Seaway").

Caravans of merchants passed close to Nazareth every day, bringing their wares from countries all around the Mediterranean. It is not hard to imagine the boy Jesus and his friends encountering these caravans, learning about the customs of other peoples, and hearing other languages spoken.

The people of Nazareth were also influenced by *Sepphoris,* the main city of the region during New Testament times. Excavations during the 1980s confirmed the fact that Sepphoris was a large and thriving city filled with different people from around the world. Because it was a little more than three miles away, Sepphoris could be seen easily from Nazareth. Even though it is never mentioned in the New Testament, Sepphoris undoubtedly affected the lives of everyone in Nazareth and the surrounding region.

It is interesting to know that Jesus lived so close to Sepphoris, only an hour's walk from his home. Did Jesus spend a great deal of time there? Probably not, because it was not a traditionally Jewish town. It was controlled by Roman forces, and perhaps it did not even have a synagogue. Whatever the case, Jesus must have walked its streets at one time or another and maybe did business there. But as far as we know, Jesus' preaching ministry was restricted to traditional Jewish towns and villages.

Many Languages

What language did Jesus learn as he grew up? His everyday language would have been Aramaic. In ancient times *Aramaic* was the common language for business and government throughout the entire area of the Near East, including Israel, Syria, and Mesopotamia. It was the language used by the common people, and this included Jesus and his family. So extensive was the use of Aramaic that it was spoken throughout the region for over a thousand years.

Open-air market

Large catch of fish, Sea of Galilee

Today when we read the New Testament, we find some Aramaic words. In Mark 5:41, for example, Jesus says to the girl whom he is restoring to life, "'*Talitha koum*,' which means, 'Little girl, I say to you, arise!'" In Mark 14:36 as well, Jesus addresses God the Father with the word *Abba*, which was a loving way of saying "Father."

Along with Aramaic Jesus knew Hebrew, the language of the ancient Israelites that was used by the Jews for worship. He would have learned Hebrew at the synagogue. Besides this Jesus would have known some Greek so that he could conduct business with foreigners from other parts of the Roman Empire. More than likely, however, he did not know Latin, which was the language of the Roman soldiers who occupied his country. All in all, Jesus' many languages served him well in his ministry: Aramaic for teaching the common people, Hebrew for speaking about the Scriptures and God's law, and Greek when speaking with others from foreign lands. Even today, knowing many languages is an important skill.

Some people may wonder why Aramaic never became the language of the New Testament, especially because it was the language of Jesus himself. The entire New Testament, in fact, was written in Greek. Why was this so? At the time of Jesus, Greek was the official language of the Roman Empire. Although the Roman language was Latin, the Romans themselves preferred Greek because they liked and imitated the Greek culture. Today we might say that Greek was the "in" language. Most important, the use of Greek by the early Church and the New Testament writers tells us that the message of Christianity quickly spread from Israel to the wider world of the Roman Empire and the world of Greek-speaking Jews and Gentiles.

How have you been influenced by your country, your culture, and your language? Give some examples.

Scripture INSIGHT

Many of the apostles are described as fishing in the Sea of Galilee. They would never have been able to fish in the Dead Sea, however, because its water is twenty-five percent salt. Nothing can live in it, and that is why it is called the Dead Sea.

Life in Nazareth

Everywhere in the world, climate affects the way people live. This was true for Jesus and the people of Nazareth. They lived in a Mediterranean climate. This influenced every aspect of their lives, from the clothes they wore to the houses in which they lived.

Clothing The climate of Israel was hot and dry, and this required the use of loose-fitting clothing. Both men and women wore tunics, long pieces of material sewn up the sides with openings for the head and arms. A belt around the waist secured the tunic and made it look neater. Most people also wore a head covering for protection from the heat of the sun. Jesus would have worn the head covering popular with the men of his day. This consisted of a square piece of cloth that fell back over the neck and was kept in place with a circle of cord. Women wore veils. Such head coverings protected a person's head, face, and neck from the sun.

Most people wore sandals because tight-fitting shoes would have made their feet hot and sore and would have been unhealthy. However, wearing sandals meant that people's feet got dirty very quickly. As a result people had to stop often and shake the dust from their feet. A sign of hospitality was to wash the feet of those who came to your home for a visit.

Housing The climate also had an influence on the way houses were built. A typical house was square and made of mud, bricks, and stone. It faced north and opened away from the heat of the sun. To keep the house cool, there were few windows. This left the interior dark, but the use of oil lamps made the houses light and comfortable.

The roof of a house was always flat; it could be used as an extra room after the sun had set. Made of branches and rolled clay, the roof could also be broken open easily. We find an example of this in Mark 2:1–12. According to Mark, Jesus was in a

Clothing typical at the time of Jesus

Contemporary folk dancing

to chess. Wrestling matches, archery contests, and footraces were also popular.

Instead of going to the pagan theaters of the Romans and Greeks, the Jews of Jesus' day listened to their own traveling storytellers and teachers. Around campfires in the desert, on rooftops in the towns, or on mountainsides, people gathered to hear the stories about their ancestors in faith and about God's love. Perhaps the best example of this type of traveling teacher was Jesus himself.

house filled with people. So great was the crowd that the roof had to be opened in order that a paralytic could be lowered in to see Jesus.

Most houses had only one story, although rich people sometimes had an upper story or room. It was in one of these upper rooms that Jesus celebrated the Last Supper. Inside, houses had dirt floors and were sparsely furnished. People sat and also slept on mats on the floor. Tables were rare; but when they were used, they were low to the ground, unlike tables today. In comparison with the lives of many modern people, Jesus and the people of his time lived in a very simple way.

Leisure Time   Living a simple way of life did not mean that people could not have fun. One of the favorite pastimes of people in Jesus' day was dancing, especially at celebrations such as weddings. This folk dancing was lively and high-spirited. It was usually accompanied with music played on flutes, horns, cymbals, and drums called timbrels. Jesus himself talked about music and dancing in the parable of the prodigal son (Luke 15:25).

Some leisure time was taken up with sports and games of the day. Young children would play games such as hide-and-seek and blindman's bluff. Older children played board games similar

For Jesus and his people, life was exciting. It was not a life of work only but was filled with music and dance, stories and song, games and sports. Far from being dull and gloomy, life was to be celebrated in praise of God, both in the family and in the larger community.

 How do you show God that life is to be celebrated?

CATHOLIC ID

The Jews of Jesus' day interpreted the first commandment literally. That is why they never carved or painted images and did not encourage the visual arts. Catholics, too, understand that images can never substitute for the one true God or be worshiped. The early Church, however, began to realize that the works of artists are powerful tools that can lead us to the worship of God and the veneration of the saints. That understanding continues today and explains why so much of the world's great art has been encouraged by the Church.

Preparing for Life

Why did Jesus become a carpenter? Why were some of his disciples fishermen? The answer is the same for each question: They received their skills from their families. In fact, the family was the real center for education at the time of Jesus.

At Home For the first few years of life, children were taught by their mothers. Each Jewish mother would teach her children how to pray and would share with them the wonderful stories about their ancestors in faith, beginning with Abraham and Sarah. Because there were no books, all this was done from memory.

After about the age of three, girls continued to be taught by their mothers. They had to learn how to plan meals according to the strict dietary laws of the Jews. They also had to learn how to cook the special dishes used for the Passover celebration and other festivities. Jewish mothers prepared their daughters for the hard task of running a home and bringing up children. This included cleaning, cooking, sewing, weaving, and mending. The girls were taught to grind the grain and make bread.

Some girls even had to help with the care of animals and with the harvest. In all aspects of life, the mother of the family prepared her daughters for the future so that eventually they, too, could be good wives and mothers.

Fathers looked after the education of their sons. Naturally a father would want to pass on what he knew to his son, especially his trade. So generally brickmakers' sons became brickmakers; shepherds' sons tended the flocks with their fathers; carpenters' sons learned how to work with wood and how to build things; merchants' sons were taught how to buy and sell goods. A boy's education took place as he worked side by side with his father.

In the New Testament Jesus is known as "the carpenter's son" (Matthew 13:55). Joseph, the foster father of Jesus, taught him the trade of carpentry. No doubt Saint Paul, who was known as a tentmaker (Acts 18:3), learned this trade from his father. Paul used this valuable skill to support himself on his journeys as he spread the good news about Jesus.

The Youth of Our Lord, John Rogers Herbert, 1847–1856

At School In addition to the education that boys received at home, it was customary for them to go to the synagogue school in their town or village. They began when they were six or seven years old and completed their studies when they were thirteen. School was not easy. Days were long, and holidays were few. At the synagogue school boys learned to read and write Hebrew, the language of the Scriptures. They would repeat the verses of Scripture until they knew them by heart. The teacher in a synagogue school was a scribe who was called a *rabbi* (teacher). Teachers were respected members of the community.

A young man who wanted to become a rabbi continued his education after age thirteen. He was sent to Jerusalem, where he studied under famous rabbis. In addition to teaching the children, a rabbi at the local synagogue taught the adults on the Sabbath. He interpreted the Scriptures and helped the people to live according to God's law. Although Jesus never studied to be a rabbi, he was given that title (John 3:2) because people, including his enemies, recognized that he was a great teacher.

Ready to Hear the Good News

The land and customs of Israel and its people were the background for the life of the greatest man who ever walked the face of the earth, Jesus of Nazareth. Knowing about geography and customs is both interesting and helpful. The more we get to know about the place and time in which Jesus lived, the more we get to know him. Such knowledge can never substitute for our faith in Jesus, the Son of God, but it fills out the picture that the gospels provide for us.

Now we are ready to turn to the good news of Jesus Christ and all that he means for us. We will be better able to understand the Jesus who sought out both rich and poor, the Jesus who healed the sick and forgave sinners, the Jesus who taught us of God's overwhelming love for us, the Jesus who saved us from sin by his death and resurrection and who changed the world forever.

 What similarities do you see between your education and the one Jesus had? Explain.

Catholic Teachings

About Respect for Others

Basing its teaching on the Ten Commandments, the Church wants us to live a life filled with respect for others. This means respect for our elders and all those in authority, whether they are members of our family or not. This respect also extends to those who are different from us, to those who are less fortunate—in fact, to every person. We find this attitude of respect in Jesus, who learned from his family, his community, and his faith. Wise people try to make this attitude part of their lives, too.

PUTTING IT TOGETHER

things
to think about

Imagine that you spend a day with Jesus in Nazareth. What would it be like?

How would you compare family life today with family life as Jesus knew it?

things
to share

In your opinion, what is the most important thing people should remember about the world in which Jesus grew up? Why?

Jesus was once your age. What would you like to ask him, if you could, about what it felt like for him?

WORDS TO REMEMBER

Find and define the following:

Aramaic _____

_____

_____

Sepphoris _____

_____

_____

OnLine
WITH THE PARISH

Different cultures contribute to the customs, music, and architecture of a local parish. What cultures have influenced your parish? See what you can find out.

Describe the land of Jesus and its regions.

1

Why would Jesus and other young people from Nazareth have known about cultures other than their own?

2

Explain one leisure activity in which Jesus may have participated.

3

How was a typical house constructed at the time of Jesus?

4

Why was the local rabbi so important for a Jewish community in Jesus' day?

5

Life in the Spirit

Imagine yourself with Jesus in his home in Nazareth. Think about Mary teaching Jesus to share some food with the hungry. Perhaps Joseph gave Jesus an example of kindness and compassion by helping a needy neighbor to build something. Spend some time thinking quietly about life with the Holy Family. How do you think they treated one another? spoke with one another? Pray that you, too, can grow in generosity, kindness, and compassion for others.

The Good News About Jesus

Praise to you,
Lord Jesus Christ.

$\mathcal{W}$hy do Catholics stand at Mass for the proclamation of the gospel? Why are the words of the gospel so important? What do you think?

Observing, Diana Ong, 1997

Gospel and Gospel

Most people know that the word *gospel* means "good news." However, many people are surprised when they find out that the word originally referred to political good news. What type of political news would be good in ancient times? News about three events in particular was cause for special celebration:

- the birth of an heir to the throne, which meant that the ruling family would continue in power
- the beginning of the reign of a new king
- the visit of a king to one of his cities.

Ancient peoples would be excited upon hearing such good news. On these happy occasions the king might pardon those accused of crimes, or he might promise that new buildings or facilities would be built for the people.

Knowing this, we can understand why the writers of the New Testament chose the word *gospel* to describe the good news of Jesus Christ. This good news was also cause for celebration:

- the incarnation and birth of God's only Son
- the bursting in of God's kingdom in its fullness in Jesus
- the arrival of the Savior bringing forgiveness of sins and salvation for the whole world.

The gospel of Jesus Christ, then, announces astonishing news. For this reason it is easy to see why Catholics stand whenever the gospel is proclaimed in the liturgy. Among all the Scriptures the gospels are our principal source for the life and teaching of Jesus. We acclaim the reading of the gospel in song, we stand when it is read, and the priest or deacon kisses the page on which the sacred words are printed. No other part of Scripture is treated in the same way.

In the New Testament the good news about Jesus is told from four different points of view: according to the views of Matthew, Mark, Luke, and John. No one should be confused by this, however. There is only one good news about Jesus, but it is told in four unique ways.

Where did the inspired words of the four gospels come from? What were their origins? Who wrote them down? We already know that the gospels came about in three stages. First there was Jesus himself; then came the Church with its oral tradition and the apostolic preaching about Jesus; and finally there came the gospels themselves, written between the late 60s and the early 90s of the first century A.D.

Because these gospels were written so many years after the time of Jesus, the writers were probably not eyewitnesses to his life and ministry. They were what we might call second-generation Christians. Guided by the Holy Spirit, they took what they had received and organized what they knew and believed about Jesus in four different ways. They did this to serve the spiritual needs of the communities for which they wrote.

One way to look at the four gospels is to consider them as four different portraits of the same Person. The four *evangelists,*

A reminder of the four different visions of the evangelists

or gospel writers, are like painters who used the same subject. Each gives us a different way of approaching Jesus, but each gives us the same truth about Jesus in the end.

This truth about Jesus is so important that the four gospels are placed first in the New Testament. But that does not mean they were written first. In fact the gospels were among the last books of the New Testament to be written. Most of the epistles, or letters, had been written long before the gospels. When Paul used the word *gospel* in his letters, he was referring simply to the good news of Jesus, not to the works of Matthew, Mark, Luke, or John.

In discussing the gospels, we should be clear about one other point. When the gospels were first written, they did not contain the names of the men who wrote them. It was only many years later that people tried to identify the evangelists by name. As we look at each gospel, we will discuss the question of its authorship. But the most important thing to remember is that each gospel account is the good news about Jesus, not the good news about Matthew, Mark, Luke, or John.

Why do you think the gospels are so important in the life of the Church?

Similar but Different

The more time we spend with the gospels, the more we discover about their unique features. What strikes us first is that the Gospels of Matthew, Mark, and Luke are very similar to one another. The Gospel of John is quite different from the other three. Why is this so?

It is obvious that the writers of the Gospels of Matthew, Mark, and Luke were especially interested in writing about the parables and miracles of Jesus. But the writer of John's Gospel put his gospel together from a different point of view. Rather than emphasizing the details of Jesus' life and ministry, he wanted to give a deeper reflection on Jesus and what he meant for the world. That is why John's writing is so much more symbolic than that of Matthew, Mark, or Luke. Put simply, John was a great thinker; Matthew, Mark, and Luke were great narrators.

If we put the Gospels of Matthew, Mark, and Luke side by side in parallel columns and look at them together, we see many similarities. That is why they are called the *synoptic gospels. Synoptic* is a word that means "looking at together." It is easy to remember the meaning of this word by recalling its Greek roots: *optic,* meaning "to see," and *syn,* meaning "together."

We can appreciate the similarities found in the synoptic gospels by comparing a few of the many parallel passages. In doing so, it is easy to see that there are many more similarities than differences. Here are several examples that are contained in all three of the synoptic gospels:

- the baptism of Jesus: Matthew 3:13–17, Mark 1:9–11, and Luke 3:21–22
- the temptation of Jesus: Matthew 4:1–11, Mark 1:12–13, and Luke 4:1–13
- the cure of Peter's mother-in-law: Matthew 8:14–15, Mark 1:29–31, and Luke 4:38–39
- the parable of the mustard seed: Matthew 13:31–32, Mark 4:30–32, and Luke 13:18–19.

Choose one example above, and compare the parallel passages. What similarities do you find? Name any differences you detect.

A Closer Look at the Synoptics

The fact that the synoptic gospels have similarities does not mean that they are exactly the same. Each writer presented a different point of view, each was directing his gospel to a different audience, and each had a different emphasis in relating the good news of Jesus.

This means that, like all ancient writers, they felt free to adapt what they knew about Jesus to their narratives. They were not worried about the exact sequence of events in Jesus' life, for example. The writers rearranged the events in order to bring out their significance more clearly. They did not change the truth; they simply put it in a different order.

The Lord's Prayer: A Synoptic Comparison

Matthew 6:9–13

Our Father in heaven,
   hallowed be your name,
   your kingdom come,
   your will be done,
      on earth as in heaven.
   Give us today our daily bread;
   and forgive us our debts,
      as we forgive our debtors;
   and do not subject us to the final test,
      but deliver us from the evil one.

Luke 11:2–4

Father, hallowed be your name,
   your kingdom come.
   Give us each day our daily bread
   and forgive us our sins
   for we ourselves forgive everyone
      in debt to us,
   and do not subject us to the
      final test.

Several passages illustrate the freedom that the synoptic writers exercised in relating the truth of the gospel. Look, for example, at the different versions of the Beatitudes in Matthew 5:3–11 and Luke 6:20–26. Matthew lists eight beatitudes, whereas Luke has only four and tells them from a completely different point of view. Which is correct? Both are correct. Both give the teaching of Jesus, but with different emphases.

In much the same way, the Lord's Prayer is different in Matthew 6:9–13 and Luke 11:1–4. The Our Father has seven petitions in Matthew and five in Luke. In Matthew's Gospel Jesus teaches the prayer in an extended version during his Sermon on the Mount. In Luke's Gospel Jesus gives the Our Father to his disciples while he himself is at prayer. These two synoptic evangelists have used the same teachings of Jesus but summarized them in their own ways; each had a different emphasis in relating the good news. (See the comparison chart above).

In telling the same stories, the synoptics sometimes change certain details. By doing so, they give us new insights into Jesus and our faith in him. In telling of the time when Jesus walked on the water, for example, the writers of Matthew and Mark end their accounts with different conclusions. In Mark the disciples

remained astonished and confused about Jesus (Mark 6:45–51). Matthew, however, concludes his account with the disciples professing their faith in Jesus as the Son of God (Matthew 14:22–33). Matthew does this in other places as well. He frequently introduces professions of faith that are not part of other gospel accounts.

 You may wish to read and compare these two accounts of Jesus walking on the water.

Now that we know the difference between the synoptic gospels and the Gospel of John, we can turn our attention to each gospel individually.

Scripture Insight

Do all the synoptic gospels—Matthew, Mark, and Luke—tell the same stories? The answer is no. Sometimes only two tell the same story; sometimes a story appears in only one gospel. Does the fact that John's Gospel occasionally has the same story as the synoptics make it a synoptic gospel, too? No. It is just too different from the other three gospels.

Mark: A Winged Lion

By comparing the gospels over the centuries, Scripture scholars have concluded that Mark's Gospel was the first to be written. The placing of Matthew as the first gospel in the New Testament is a custom that came from the early Church and that continues today. But Mark was written first.

The author of the Gospel of Mark is not mentioned in the gospel itself; however, he is generally considered to be John Mark, who is mentioned in Acts 12:12. We know that Mark was the cousin of Barnabas, the traveling companion of Saint Paul. Mark was at Paul's side during his imprisonment by the Romans (Colossians 4:10). Later Mark was also with Peter in Rome (1 Peter 5:13).

Mark's association with Peter and Paul helps scholars to assign a date to his writing. They have concluded that the Gospel of Mark was written somewhere between A.D. 65 and 70. As a disciple of Peter, Mark may have written his gospel in Rome. In any case it seems clear that he was a Jewish Christian who wrote for a Gentile audience. One clue to this is that he takes the time to translate Aramaic words and expressions and to explain Jewish customs.

Because his gospel was the first to be written, Mark is credited with inventing the gospel literary form. Even though Mark's Gospel is the shortest of the four, it still tells the good news with excitement, using lively and vivid words. It almost seems that Mark is bringing us along to walk side by side with Jesus. Some people say that his portrait of Jesus was influenced by Peter the apostle, who was Jesus' constant companion on his travels through Palestine. Reading Mark is like seeing Jesus through the eyes of Peter.

What do we learn about Jesus from Mark? Mark wants us to know that Jesus is the suffering Messiah. We also learn that Jesus asks his disciples for a radical change in their lives. That would not always be easy, and it could even involve suffering. How should Jesus' disciples bear this hardship? Mark's answer is that they should look to the cross and their crucified Lord. Jesus, who suffered and died for us, shows us that we, too, must be faithful, even during suffering.

The traditional symbol for the writer of Mark's Gospel is a winged desert lion. It was chosen because this gospel opens with the voice of John the Baptist crying out in the desert wilderness.

Matthew: A Winged Human

Scholars think that the author of Matthew's Gospel was also a Jewish Christian. He probably was a scribe, a teacher familiar with Jewish customs and everything that had to do with the Jewish religion. In his gospel he taught as a true rabbi, directing his writing to a Jewish audience. That is why his writing is filled with typical Jewish expressions. For example, Matthew was the only one of the synoptic gospel writers to speak of the kingdom of heaven, rather than the kingdom of God. The reason for this is that out of reverence the Jews did not pronounce the divine name.

**Mark, painting by Tissot
19th century**

So familiar was the writer with his Jewish roots that he placed more than 130 references to the Old Testament in his gospel. A clue to the writer's identity as a Jewish scribe may come from Matthew 13:52, where Matthew writes, "Every scribe who has been instructed in the kingdom of heaven is like the head of a household who brings from his storeroom both the new and the old."

From all that we know, this gospel was written between A.D. 70 and 90. A careful reading of Matthew tells us that he was familiar with Mark's Gospel. He also knew that the Temple of Jerusalem no longer existed; the Temple had been destroyed in A.D. 70. Matthew's Gospel is later and comes from a community that had more time to reflect on Jesus and what he meant for the Church. Matthew is the only one of the four gospels in which the word *church* is actually used; it is also the only gospel concerned with the Church's organization (Matthew 16:18; 18:17).

Matthew's Gospel contains more of Jesus' sayings than the other gospels. That is why some people have compared it with a type of catechism, useful for teaching. For these and other reasons, this gospel has for centuries been called the Church's gospel. It has always been held in high esteem and was the most frequently quoted of the gospels.

Matthew, painting by Tissot 19th century

Who is Jesus for Matthew? Jesus is the fulfillment of all God's promises that came down through Moses and the prophets. Jesus is now the great lawgiver and teacher. He is the new Moses, described as giving the famous Sermon on the Mount (Matthew 5—7). Jesus did this just as Moses taught God's law from Mount Sinai.

The traditional symbol for the writer of Matthew's Gospel is a winged human figure. It was chosen because this gospel begins with the genealogy, or listing, of Jesus' human ancestors.

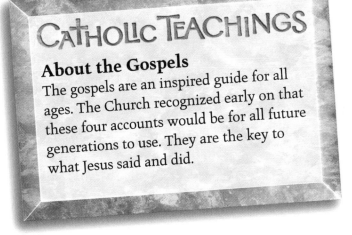

CATHOLIC TEACHINGS

About the Gospels

The gospels are an inspired guide for all ages. The Church recognized early on that these four accounts would be for all future generations to use. They are the key to what Jesus said and did.

What is the most surprising thing you have learned about the Gospels of Mark and Matthew? Explain.

Luke, painting by Tissot, 19th century

Luke: The Winged Ox

The Gospel of Luke is unusual among the four gospel accounts because it is probably the only one written by a Gentile rather than by a Jew. Ever since the second century, the author of Luke has been identified with the "beloved physician" of Colossians 4:14. Because this gospel is written in somewhat polished Greek, we know that the writer must have been well educated. His home was probably Antioch in Syria, the third-largest city of the Roman Empire in the first century.

Why did Luke write his gospel? For one thing, we know that he was an early companion of Saint Paul. This meant that he knew a great deal about Jesus and his teachings. But more important, he was involved in missionary work to the Gentiles and became sensitive to the needs of converts from paganism. With his writing ability and his missionary experiences, he was well suited to share his understanding of the gospel message with other Gentiles. He wanted them to know that Jesus was the Savior of the whole world, including both Jews and Gentiles.

One of the most interesting facts about Luke is that his gospel is the first book of a two-volume work: the gospel itself and the Acts of the Apostles. When we look at the beginning of each of these books (Luke 1:3; Acts 1:1), we see that Luke addresses both of them to the same person, Theophilus, whose name means "lover of God." Luke wanted Theophilus and every other lover of God to "realize the certainty of the teachings" they had received (Luke 1:4).

Luke probably wrote his gospel between A.D. 80 and 85. What portrait of Jesus does he give us? Luke's Jesus is filled with mercy and compassion. He cares for everyone but shows a special tenderness for the afflicted and oppressed. This includes sinners, the poor, and outcasts. Think of the parable of the Good Samaritan, which is found only in this gospel (Luke 10:29–37). Jesus' identification with the lowly goes even further. He respects everyone and defends the dignity of all. He is especially sensitive to women. In fact Luke presents many stories of women not found in the other gospels.

The traditional symbol for the writer of Luke's Gospel is a winged ox. Oxen were sacrificial animals. This symbol was chosen because Luke's Gospel begins with Zechariah, the father of John the Baptist, offering a sacrifice in the Temple.

John: A Soaring Eagle

When the Church wants to express its deepest belief in Jesus, it turns to one gospel only: the Gospel of John. This is made clear when we look at the major celebrations of the liturgical year. At Christmas Mass During the Day, we hear the beginning of John's Gospel. At the Holy Thursday Evening Mass of the Lord's Supper, John's account of the washing of the feet is read each year. On Good Friday we join in proclaiming the account of Jesus' passion and death according to John.

On Easter Sunday we sing alleluia before hearing John's Gospel. Selections from this gospel are heard during most of the Easter season and always on Pentecost Sunday. Truly the Church must see something tremendously important for us in John's Gospel to have chosen it so often.

Does the Church's choice indicate that John's Gospel is better than that of Matthew, Mark, or Luke? Of course not. All four are part of God's inspired word. What it does tell us, however, is that John is different from the synoptics. This gospel soars to the heights of reflection. As mentioned before, John is not interested in simply giving us the narrative of Jesus' life and ministry. His primary interest is to give us a deeper insight into the meaning of Jesus' words and deeds. That is why he uses so many symbols and writes in such a beautiful and poetic way.

This picturesque language is evident very early on in the gospel when Jesus is called the Lamb of God (John 1:29). Other examples include the time when Jesus is named the Bread of Life (John 6:35) and the Good Shepherd (John 10:11). Language such as this has also led scholars to date this gospel as the last one, written between A.D. 90 and 100.

Who wrote this magnificent gospel? Many people have thought it was the apostle John. However, because it was written so many years after the death and resurrection of Jesus, its author was most likely a Jewish disciple or disciples of some eyewitness to Jesus. That eyewitness could very well have been the apostle John.

The traditional symbol for the writer of John's Gospel is a soaring eagle. It was chosen because of the sublime and majestic content of this gospel. Readers of this gospel often feel as if they, too, are eagles soaring high into the sky.

What is the most surprising thing you have learned about the Gospels of Luke and John?

John, painting by Tissot
19th century

CATHOLIC ID The symbols for the four evangelists were suggested by the imagery found in the first chapter of the prophet Ezekiel. These four symbols—the winged lion, the winged human figure, the winged ox, and the soaring eagle—have been used in Church art and architecture for many centuries.

things to think about

Suppose that the gospels had never been written. Where would we find out about Jesus?

Imagine that you have written a gospel. How would people describe your point of view about Jesus and the good news?

things to share

Someone says to you, "Now that I've read one gospel, I don't need to bother with the other three. After all, they are all the same." What would you say?

From what you have studied about the four evangelists, which gospel would you want to read first?

WORDS TO REMEMBER

Find and define the following:

evangelists _____
_____
_____

synoptic gospels _____
_____
_____

OnLine WITH THE PARISH

Very often the book of the gospels used at Mass has a beautiful covering of cloth or metal. Many centuries ago it was the custom to decorate these covers with precious jewels. How does your parish show its love and respect for the gospels?

Name some similarities and differences among the synoptic gospels.

1

If Mark was the first gospel writer, why is his book not placed first in the New Testament?

2

Identify the writer of Matthew's Gospel, and tell why he probably wrote after A.D. 70.

3

Name and explain the symbol for the writer of Luke's Gospel.

4

Life *in the Spirit*

During the liturgical year the Church remembers one of the four evangelists each day when a gospel selection is read at Mass. The Church sets aside one day to honor each of them: Mark on April 25, Matthew on September 21, Luke on October 18, and John on December 27. Plan some way that you, too, can honor the evangelists on their feast days. Perhaps you can spend more time reading from their gospel accounts.

Why does the Church turn to the Gospel of John when it wants to express its deepest belief in Jesus?

5

CHAPTER 7

The Only
Son of God

For God all things are possible.

Matthew 19:26

*W*henever heads of state travel anywhere in the world, preparations must be made to assure the success of their visit. Advance teams see to every detail in anticipation of their arrival. The way is made as smooth as possible. What kind of an "advance team" do you think God sent to prepare the way for his only Son?

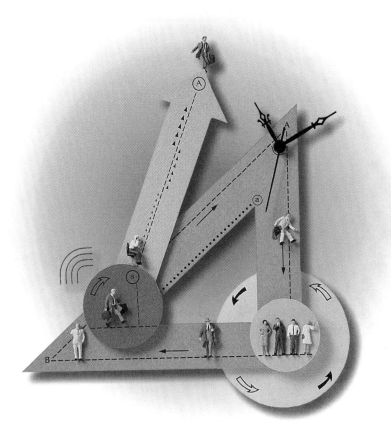

God's Advance Team

Most advance teams are made up of many people. Some of them look after security details; others prepare for meetings or important events. But there was just one person on God's advance team for the coming of Jesus. That person was John the Baptist. He was the one whom God had chosen to prepare the way for his only Son.

John the Baptist has always been one of the most interesting characters of the New Testament. He must have been important for the early Church because he is mentioned many times in all four gospel accounts. In fact even Josephus, the first-century Jewish historian, mentions that John had a powerful influence over the people during the time of Jesus (*Antiquities*, 18).

The information we have about John's birth and infancy comes to us from the Gospel of Luke. We learn that John's parents, Zechariah and Elizabeth, were elderly and had not been able to have children. Zechariah was a poor country priest who took his turn going to the Temple in Jerusalem to perform his priestly duties. It was on one such occasion that the angel Gabriel appeared to him. Gabriel told Zechariah that his wife, Elizabeth, would now give birth to a son in her old age. This divine messenger also said that the boy's name was to be John, a name meaning "God is gracious."

When we read the account of John's birth in Luke 1:5–25, we notice that many details are similar to the birth accounts of famous people in the Old Testament. All these accounts include some of the following details:

- a child born of aged parents
- a mother who previously had not been able to bear children
- the birth made possible only through God's intervention and sometimes announced by heavenly messengers
- the child's name given by a heavenly messenger.

Like Elizabeth, the mothers of these famous Old Testament people were advanced in age or had not been able to bear children. Sometimes the births of their children were announced by a heavenly messenger, or the children were given divinely appointed names. These great biblical women include:

- Sarah, the wife of Abraham and mother of Isaac (Genesis 17:15–19)
- Rebekah, the wife of Isaac and mother of Jacob and Esau (Genesis 25:21)
- Rachel, the wife of Jacob and mother of Joseph and Benjamin (Genesis 29:31; 30:22–24)
- the wife of Manoah and mother of Samson (Judges 13:1–25)
- Hannah, the wife of Elkanah and mother of Samuel (1 Samuel 1:1—2:11).

Luke was well acquainted with these birth accounts. In a masterful way he used his skills as an evangelist to remind us of them and of the way God worked in the lives of our ancestors in faith. He did this to show that the son of Zechariah and Elizabeth

was also to be important for God's people. But even though the story of John's birth was similar to those of the births of other important individuals, it was still unique. That is because John was "filled with the holy Spirit even from his mother's womb" (Luke 1:15). This happened when Mary, the mother of Jesus, visited Elizabeth at the time both of them were pregnant.

Luke's Gospel records that during this visitation, John leaped for joy in his mother's womb because of the presence of Jesus (Luke 1:41). The powerful presence of the Savior of the world was felt even before he was born! The Church remembers this in the preface of the Mass used on the two feasts of Saint John the Baptist. The priest prays to God:

> You set John the Baptist apart from other men,
> marking him out with special favor.
> His birth brought great rejoicing:
> even in the womb he leapt for joy,
> so near was man's salvation.

Why would Mary, the mother of Jesus, visit Elizabeth? Because they were cousins. John the Baptist and Jesus, therefore, were related to each other. According to Luke, John was six months older than Jesus.

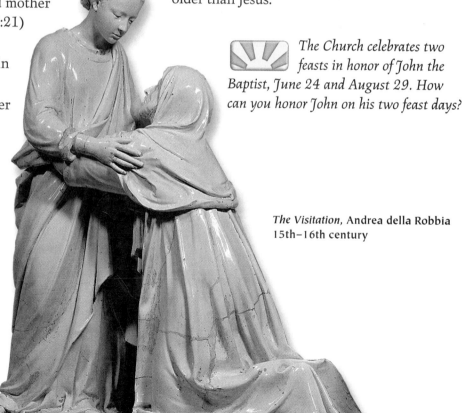

The Church celebrates two feasts in honor of John the Baptist, June 24 and August 29. How can you honor John on his two feast days?

The Visitation, Andrea della Robbia 15th–16th century

Detail from *The Story of John the Baptist*,
Fra Filippo Lippi, 15th century

Bridging the Testaments

When John the Baptist was a young boy, people probably thought he would be a priest as his father was. After all, the priesthood of the Old Testament was hereditary, and sons usually followed in their fathers' footsteps. But God had different plans for John, plans that would surprise everyone. John would be described by the gospel writers as "a voice of one crying out in the desert" (Mark 1:3). Why was he in the desert? What was it that God wanted him to do? John was to be a precursor, a preacher, and a prophet.

Precursor For centuries the Jews had been waiting for the Savior promised by God. John was the one chosen to announce the Savior's coming. That is why John is called the precursor of the

Lord. A *precursor* is a "forerunner," someone who comes immediately before another person and indicates that person's approach.

John the Baptist had gone out to the desert. There he readied himself to be the precursor of the Lord Jesus and to prepare his way. Everything about John—the food he ate, the severe way he lived, even the clothes he wore—alerted people to the fact that something new was about to happen (Mark 1:6). A man with a powerful personality and outstanding in holiness, John attracted many disciples. He did this, however, not for himself but to tell them, "One mightier than I is coming after me. I am not worthy to stoop and loosen the thongs of his sandals" (Mark 1:7).

Preacher When John spoke to the people, he spoke about repentance. He told them that they must turn away from sin and reform their lives. In this way they would get themselves ready for the Lord's coming. As a sign of their willingness to change their lives, many people were baptized by John in the Jordan River. Of course this was not our sacrament of Baptism; it was, rather, a sign of repentance. Even Jesus himself underwent this baptism by John, but not because he had to repent for sins. Jesus did it to show the people that what John was asking of them was correct and true. It was also at this moment that Jesus began his public life. After Jesus' baptism by John, "the heavens were opened," and the Holy Spirit came upon Jesus in the form of a dove. Then Jesus heard a voice saying, "This is my beloved Son, with whom I am well pleased" (Matthew 3:16–17).

The day that Jesus went to the Jordan River to be baptized, John pointed him out to the people. John said, "Behold, the Lamb of God, who takes away the sin of the world" (John 1:29). The Baptist was letting the people know that Jesus was the long-awaited Savior, who would save them from their sins. John's task was complete. Now he could say of himself and of Jesus, "He must increase; I must decrease" (John 3:30). There was no question in John's mind that his job was to point other people to Jesus, not to himself.

Prophet A *prophet* is one called by God to speak for him. Certainly John was a prophet, the "prophet of the Most High" (Luke 1:76). In fact the Church teaches that "John surpasses all the prophets, of whom he is the last" (*Catechism*, 523). That is why we say that John is the bridge between the Old and New Testaments. He is the last of the Old Testament prophets and the first to announce the coming of the only Son of God.

John's life was not an easy one, but he never gave up. His response to God's call and his witness to Christ eventually cost him his life. The ideals that he preached brought him many enemies; some people thought he was demanding too much. King Herod, for one, was afraid of John and his message. That is why he had John imprisoned and beheaded.

John had fearlessly denounced the sinful marriage between Herod and his brother's wife (Matthew 14:3–12). Each year the Church remembers the martyrdom of John the Baptist on August 29.

Even today the work of John the Baptist is not finished. He is a model for the Church as we prepare for Christ's second coming. For this reason John is an important figure during the Advent season. Just as John helped the world to prepare for the coming of Jesus into our world, so he helps us to renew our hope and expectation that Christ will come again.

Jesus himself said that John the Baptist was "a burning and shining lamp" (John 5:35). Now that John has pointed out the way for us, we are ready to turn to the greatest moment in human history, the birth of the Messiah, the Savior of the world.

 What example does John the Baptist give us? How can we follow that example?

Scripture INSIGHT

At the time of John the Baptist, a type of monastic community of Jews lived in the desert on the shore of the Dead Sea. These were the Essenes. They lived in the desert apart from other Jews and were awaiting the coming of God's kingdom. The Essenes felt that this was the only way to live the law of Moses perfectly and were critical of other Jews, whom they considered lax. John probably encountered the Essenes in the desert and was familiar with their teachings. Unlike the Essenes, however, John went out of the desert to preach. Our knowledge of the Essenes increased a great deal when the Dead Sea scrolls were discovered in a cave near the Dead Sea in 1947. The place of this archaeological discovery is called Qumran.

The Infancy Narratives

Some people think they know all about the birth of Jesus and the wonderful events surrounding the coming of the Messiah. But when they read the biblical accounts of his birth, they are surprised to learn that these accounts are deeper and much richer than they ever imagined.

The first thing a reader of the New Testament will notice is that only the Gospels of Matthew and Luke contain the infancy narratives. The *infancy narratives* are the accounts of Jesus' conception, birth, and infancy. These accounts occur nowhere else in the New Testament, not even in the Gospels of Mark and John.

Why is this so? The earliest community of the Church was at first more interested in Jesus' passion, death, and resurrection than they were in the details of his birth. That is why Mark's Gospel and all the New Testament letters make no reference to the birth of Jesus. It was only when the community had time to reflect on Jesus' life that they began to take a greater interest in the details of his birth and infancy.

The Two Accounts

When we read the infancy narratives in Matthew 1:1—2:23 and in Luke 1:5—2:52, we see that the story of Jesus' birth is told from two points of view. Matthew tells it from Joseph's point of view, and Luke from Mary's. When we compare the two accounts, we find that each contains the following details:

- Jesus was born during the reign of King Herod the Great.
- Jesus was to be born of a virgin mother. This virgin was Mary, who was betrothed (engaged) to Joseph.
- Joseph came from the house of David. This meant that he was a descendant of King David, the famous king of Israel.
- Jesus also shared in this heritage. He, too, was a son of David.
- The birth of Jesus was announced by an angel.
- Jesus was conceived through the power of the Holy Spirit. He did not have a human father as other children do.
- The name Jesus was given to Mary and Joseph by the angel, who also said that Jesus was going to be the Savior of the world.
- Jesus was born in Bethlehem and grew up in Nazareth.

While agreeing on the main points that surround the birth of Jesus, the evangelists Matthew and Luke did not hesitate to add their own particular details to the infancy narratives. Because the evangelists were writing for different audiences, each was free to tell the story of Jesus in his own unique way.

As we know, Matthew was a Jewish Christian writing for other Jewish Christians. That is why he frequently used Old Testament terms and ideas familiar to his readers. He began his infancy narrative with a genealogy that traced Jesus' ancestry all the way back to Abraham.

For Matthew, Jesus was the new Moses. Just as Moses brought his people to freedom from slavery in Egypt, so Jesus would save all people and free them from the slavery of sin. To make this comparison clear, Matthew told the story of the Holy Family's flight into Egypt. Their escape took place as King Herod began to search for and kill all the male children in Bethlehem. In doing so, Herod hoped to eliminate any rival to his throne. It was only after his death that the Holy Family left Egypt and returned to Nazareth. Matthew's account parallels two Old Testament accounts: the Egyptian pharaoh killing the newborn male children at the time of the birth of Moses (Exodus 1:15–22) and Moses leading the Israelites out of Egypt (Exodus 13:17–22).

Matthew also recognized Jesus as the newborn king of the Jews, the Messiah descended from King David. That is one reason why his gospel has the magi coming to adore Jesus and offering him gifts of gold, frankincense, and myrrh. These were precious gifts, worthy of a king. Through the magi, Gentiles who were led to Jesus, Matthew showed that Jesus came for all people, that he had a universal mission.

Unlike Matthew, who wrote for a Jewish audience, Luke was writing for Gentiles. He wanted them to know that Jesus was the Savior of the whole world. He begins with the announcement and birth of John the Baptist. He also relates Mary's visit to Elizabeth, who immediately recognizes Jesus as the world's Savior. In Luke we meet the shepherds and hear the angelic chorus announcing Jesus' birth. We also meet Simeon and Anna in the Temple. They, too, realize that the Savior had now come into the world as God had promised.

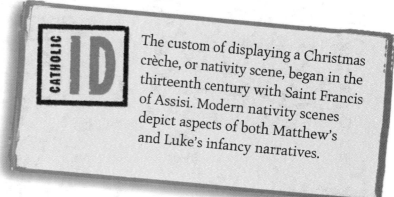

Flight into Egypt, Murillo, 17th century

 *Why do you think it was important for Matthew and Luke to include infancy narratives in their gospels?*

Good News in Miniature

For those who are willing to go more deeply into them, the infancy narratives provide more than an introduction to the Gospels of Matthew and Luke. They are in a true sense the good news of our salvation in miniature. These narratives show God's plan of salvation at work from the time of Abraham to its fulfillment and completion in Jesus Christ, the Savior of the world. Each narrative in its own way tells the truth of the incarnation of the only Son of God: The Son of God became one of us. Each wraps this truth in the beautiful imagery of the Old Testament.

Many details of the infancy narratives can be found in the Old Testament. The evangelists wove these details into their texts through the skillful use of two literary forms: genealogy and midrash. We have already studied these forms in Chapter 3. Let's look more closely at each of these to help us understand even more fully the beautiful details of the infancy narratives.

Genealogy A genealogy is a listing of ancestors, a family tree. Matthew begins his gospel and infancy narrative by proclaiming that Jesus is the son of Abraham and the son of David. By tracing Jesus' ancestry to Abraham and David, Matthew was making it perfectly clear that Jesus was the fulfillment of Israel's history. He was the Messiah, whom people expected to come from the family of David, the first king of Israel.

The first thing one notices after reading this genealogy of Jesus is that it falls into three parts. The first part deals with the patriarchs and other early ancestors of the Jews, beginning with Abraham. The second part names kings of Israel, beginning with King David. The third part lists many unknown people whose names (with the exception of the first two) were never mentioned in the Old Testament. Who are all these people in the genealogy? They include the saintly and the sinful, people of great virtue and people of great vice, even people who were unknown. By including all different kinds of people, the evangelist shows that Jesus' ancestors were just like those of the rest of humanity.

CATHOLIC TEACHINGS

About Mary's Virginity

When we say that Mary was a virgin, we mean that she never had sexual relations. Jesus was conceived through the power of the Holy Spirit. The Church teaches that Mary was a virgin before, during, and after the birth of Jesus. She was a virgin her entire life. The belief in Mary's virginity is reflected in both infancy narratives.

The genealogy includes another interesting feature. Five women are named as part of Jesus' ancestry, even though it was not customary to name women at all. In addition to Mary, the mother of Jesus, the other four are Tamar, Rahab, Ruth, and Uriah's wife, Bathsheba. Certainly Ruth was a well-loved woman in Israel's history and the great-grandmother of King David. But Rahab was a prostitute. Why would Matthew put such opposites together? Because he wanted us to realize that Jesus' ancestry was truly human and included all kinds of people. Also because Jesus came to save everyone, not just the saintly. What a skillful and masterful way for Matthew to teach us this important truth!

Midrash Through the use of midrash, the gospel writers remind their readers of familiar incidents and ideas from the Old Testament. In our study of literary forms, we have already seen one example of midrash in Matthew 2:16–23. By his reinterpretation of Jeremiah 31:15–17, Matthew shows that Jesus relived the experiences of the Jewish people.

Another example of midrash is the account of the magi's visit, found in Matthew 2:1–12, which also reinterprets several Old Testament passages. In Matthew's account the magi follow a star, the star mentioned in Numbers 24:17. The gifts the magi bring were first mentioned in Psalm 72:10 and 15 and in Isaiah 60:6. Most people do not realize that when they put up their family nativity scene, they are actually looking at elements that come from both the Old and the New Testaments.

There is so much to reflect on in both infancy narratives. But one last word should be said about the conclusion of Luke's infancy narrative. There Luke writes about Jesus being found in the Temple at the age of twelve. Jesus says to Mary and Joseph, "Why were you looking for me? Did you not know that I must be in my Father's house?" (Luke 2:49). This is the first time in this gospel that Jesus speaks, and he identifies God as his Father. The divinity and humanity of Jesus are clearly proclaimed throughout the entire infancy narratives, but these narratives conclude with a powerful declaration from Jesus' own lips that he is more than human: Jesus is a divine Person, the only Son of God.

Do you think that you might be able to identify any other gospel passages using these literary forms? Try the third chapter of Luke's Gospel.

PUTTING IT TOGETHER

things to think about

Why is it important to understand that John the Baptist is the bridge between the Old and the New Testaments?

John the Baptist said, "Behold, the Lamb of God, who takes away the sin of the world" (John 1:29). Where do we hear these words today?

things to share

Someone says to you, "Why do we have to spend so much time on John the Baptist? After all, he wasn't that important." What would you say?

What do you think is the most admirable quality of John the Baptist? What words of his will you remember?

WORDS TO REMEMBER

Find and define the following:

precursor _____

_____

_____

infancy narratives _____

_____

_____

OnLine WITH THE PARISH

Many parishes have beautiful nativity sets that are on display during the Christmas season. Perhaps this year you and a group of friends could volunteer to help in setting it up and taking it down. Some volunteers may also wish to help young children put on a nativity pageant.

1

Name two ways in which the account of the birth of John the Baptist was similar to the birth accounts of important people in the Old Testament.

2

Why did John the Baptist surpass all the prophets, of whom he was the last?

3

After reading Matthew's infancy narrative, why can we say that Jesus was the new Moses?

4

Why can we say that the infancy narratives of Matthew and Luke are like the good news in miniature?

5

Name and explain one way the literary form of midrash is used in the infancy narratives.

Life
in the Spirit

According to Luke's Gospel, John the Baptist was born six months before Jesus. That is why the Church celebrates the feast of the Birth of John the Baptist on June 24 each year, six months before Christmas. Saint Augustine thought that this June date was very appropriate. This is because John's feast day occurs after the summer solstice, the time of year when the days begin to grow shorter. The celebration of Jesus' birth occurs after the winter solstice, when the days begin to grow longer. At both times of the year, we can make John the Baptist's words our own: "He must increase; I must decrease" (John 3:30).

CHAPTER 8

Christ the Lord

To whom shall we go?
You have the words of eternal life.

John 6:68

Two thousand years ago many wandering preachers walked the hills of Israel and visited its villages and towns. What made Jesus of Nazareth different from them?

Human God and Divine Human

What made Jesus different was that he was both human and divine. At the incarnation the second Person of the Blessed Trinity became Man. He took on our human nature in every way except one: sin. John's Gospel speaks about the incarnation by saying that the Word of God, who had existed from all eternity, became flesh:

> In the beginning was the Word,
>   and the Word was with God,
>   and the Word was God. . . .
> And the Word became flesh
>   and made his dwelling among us.
> John 1:1, 14

Jesus was the Word made flesh. Could people tell that Jesus was a divine Person simply by looking at him? No. Jesus looked and lived just like everyone else. The gospels remind us that he had to eat and sleep. He knew what it was to experience joy and suffering. He had to work and pray. That is because Jesus was both human and divine. The Church proclaims this truth by teaching that he is a divine Person with two natures: a human nature and a divine nature. For this reason we can describe Jesus as the human God and the divine human.

When the Word of God, the second Person of the Blessed Trinity, became one of us at the incarnation, something truly wonderful happened:

The invisible God became visible. In Jesus we would begin to see who God really is because Jesus would reveal this to us. And what did Jesus reveal? He revealed that God is a Trinity of Persons. God is Father, Son, and Holy Spirit. Jesus is the Father's Son, the Son of God. It is very important for us to understand this relationship of Jesus to the Father. Let's take a closer look at the way it is described in the New Testament.

The author of John's Gospel made it clear that Jesus revealed his Father to us in a completely new and unique way. He let us know that God is not just the creator of the universe, who is worshiped by many people in many religions. God is uniquely Jesus' Father. This is what we learn from John's Gospel:

- Only the Son has seen the Father: "Everyone who listens to my Father and learns from him comes to me. Not that anyone has seen the Father except the one who is from God; he has seen the Father" (6:45–46).
- The Son came from the Father: "I came from God and am here; I did not come on my own, but he sent me" (8:42).
- The Son returns to the Father: "Now I am leaving the world and going back to the Father" (16:28).
- The Father is glorified in the Son and always hears the Son: "Whatever you ask in my name, I will do, so that the Father may be glorified in the Son. If you ask anything of me in my name, I will do it" (14:13–14).

- The Son has made known what he heard from the Father: "I have called you friends, because I have told you everything I have heard from my Father" (15:15).

Imagine what it was like for Jesus' disciples and others to hear God spoken about in this way! They must have been shocked to hear someone identify himself so closely with God. After all, these were Jews who had struggled for many centuries to maintain their belief in the one true God.

Of course, Jesus was not talking about many gods. He was speaking about himself and his Father, two Persons of the Blessed Trinity. At other times Jesus also spoke about the third Person of the Blessed Trinity: "The Advocate, the holy Spirit that the Father will send in my name—he will teach you everything and remind you of all that [I] told you" (John 14:26).

Father, Son, and Holy Spirit is the language that Jesus used in revealing his own identity and that of the other Persons of the Blessed Trinity. This is the language we find in the New Testament. The truth about God that Jesus revealed cannot be changed. The three Persons of the Trinity are Father, Son, and Holy Spirit. They are the three Persons in the one God. That is why we are baptized in the *name* of the Father, and of the Son, and of the Holy Spirit—and in no other name.

 In what way is your attitude toward Jesus different from your attitude toward other great heroes of history?

Meeting Jesus

If we are willing to spend time with the New Testament, especially the gospels, we have the opportunity to really meet Jesus. Not only can we find his teachings and the challenges he offers his disciples, but we are also introduced to Jesus himself. We can discover what Jesus wants us to know about him.

One day Jesus was in the Temple, and a group of people gathered around him. They were wondering who he was and wanted to know more about him. Jesus replied to their questions and told them, "The Father and I are one" (John 10:30). Another time he said, "The Father is in me and I am in the Father" (John 10:38). Through these astonishing words we learn more than the fact that Jesus is the Son of God. We learn that Jesus shared the same divinity as God the Father.

Jesus made this even clearer at other times when he spoke about himself. Some of his most memorable statements contain the words *I am*. When Jesus spoke these words, his listeners could make an immediate connection to words of the Old Testament. In the Book of Exodus, for example,

God revealed himself to Moses by saying, "This is what you shall tell the Israelites: I AM sent me to you" (Exodus 3:14). In Hebrew, the language of the Old Testament, Yahweh was God's name. *Yahweh* means "I AM."

The people around Jesus would also know from the Old Testament that God identified himself in other ways, saying such things as, "It is I," "Fear not," and "Do not be afraid." Jesus used these same expressions to comfort his disciples. By using the language of Yahweh from the Old Testament, Jesus was revealing his relationship to the Father, who loved and cared for his people.

Study the chart. Notice how often Jesus used the same language that Yahweh (God) used in the Old Testament.

One day Jesus was preaching in the Temple. The people asked him whether he was greater than their father, Abraham, or the prophets. Jesus surprised them by saying, "Amen, amen, I say to you, before Abraham came to be, I AM" (John 8:58). This was a startling statement. At the time of Jesus, Abraham would have been dead almost two thousand years!

Jesus was saying that he existed before Abraham. Because he used the divine name, I AM, the people picked up stones to throw at him. They thought Jesus was blaspheming by identifying himself with God.

As the chart makes clear, there are several types of "I am" statements that were spoken by Jesus. When we see an "I am" statement in capital letters, we know that it refers to the divine name. The other "I am" statements in the chart are descriptions Jesus gave of himself and his divine mission. Jesus, who is one with the Father, was able to reveal the Father in a unique way.

CATHOLIC ID

In Catholic churches we often see the alpha and omega, A and Ω, which are symbols for Christ. Alpha and omega are the names of the first and last letters of the Greek alphabet. In the last book of the Bible, Jesus says, "I am the Alpha and the Omega, the first and the last, the beginning and the end" (Revelation 22:12). These same words were the words God had spoken of himself in Isaiah 41:4. Jesus is truly the first and the last, the beginning and the end. He is the only Son of the Father. He is divine.

Jesus Speaks About Himself

Statements About Himself		Old Testament Background
John 6:20	"It is I. Do not be afraid."	Exodus 3:14; 6:6–8; Isaiah 41:4–10; 43:1–3, 10–13, 25; 45:18; 46:4; 48:12
John 8:24	"If you do not believe that I AM, you will die in your sins."	
John 8:28	"When you lift up the Son of Man, then you will realize that I AM."	
John 8:58	"Amen, amen, I say to you, before Abraham came to be, I AM."	
John 13:19	"From now on I am telling you before it happens, so that when it happens you may believe that I AM."	

Descriptions of Himself		Old Testament Background
John 6:35	"I am the bread of life."	Exodus 13:21; 16:4; Deuteronomy 32:39; Psalm 24:7–10; Isaiah 5:1–7; 40:11, 27–29; 41:4
John 8:12	"I am the light of the world."	
John 10:9	"I am the gate."	
John 10:11	"I am the good shepherd."	
John 11:25	"I am the resurrection and the life."	
John 14:6	"I am the way and the truth and the life."	
John 15:1	"I am the true vine."	
Revelation 22:12	"I am the Alpha and the Omega, the first and the last, the beginning and the end."	

Paralyzed Man Lowered Through the Roof, Tissot, 19th century

Authority to Forgive Sins

Jesus not only told us about his divinity; he also showed us by his actions that he was divine. One very important way he did this was by forgiving sins. An example can be seen in Mark 2:1–12. One day a crowd gathered in the house where Jesus was staying. There were so many people that no one else could come through the door. When a paralytic, a paralyzed man, was brought to see Jesus, the man's friends could not get him into the house. Instead they opened up the roof and slowly lowered the man down on a mat to see Jesus.

When Jesus saw the faith of the people, he said to the paralyzed man, "Your sins are forgiven." Some of those present were scandalized and accused Jesus of blasphemy. They said, "Who but God alone can forgive sins?"

Jesus knew what they were thinking. In order to show that he had authority to forgive sins, he said to the paralyzed man, "I say to you, rise, pick up your mat, and go home." Immediately the man got up. As he walked away, the crowd exclaimed, "We have never seen anything like this." They knew that only God could forgive sins. By his actions Jesus was letting them know that he had authority to forgive sins and was, therefore, divine. His divine power extended not only to the forgiveness of sins but to the working of miracles as well.

By showing his divinity in these ways, Jesus was not denying his humanity. But he did want to let people know that God had come into the world in a new and dramatic way. Jesus brought God's mercy and forgiveness to all people. And in doing so, Jesus let everyone know that he was the Messiah and Lord.

Messiah and Lord

God's people had been waiting a long time for the promised Savior. He would come to set them free from oppression and bring them into a whole new relationship with God. Over the centuries some people began to think of the Savior, or Messiah, as a warrior or political leader. They forgot the words of the prophets, who spoke of the Messiah as the one who would lead the people to God and guide them in the ways of justice. That is one reason why so many did not recognize Jesus as the Messiah.

What does the word *messiah* mean? It is a Hebrew word that means "the anointed one." In ancient times kings, priests, and prophets were anointed with oil as a sign of their special roles in the world. Just think of David, who was anointed by Samuel and became the greatest king of Israel. The Savior, however, was to be greater than David. The Savior would be the most important person ever to come into the world. One day a Samaritan woman said to Jesus, "I know that the Messiah is coming, the one called the Anointed; when he comes, he will tell us everything." After she said this, Jesus replied, "I am he, the one who is speaking with you" (John 4:25, 26).

Jesus is the promised Messiah. The New Testament, written in Greek, used the word *christos,* or Christ, to translate the word *messiah.* When we say Jesus Christ, therefore, we are not using *Christ* as Jesus' family name. It is his title. When we say Jesus Christ, we are really saying Jesus the Christ, or Jesus the Messiah, or Jesus the Anointed One. All three mean the same thing.

There is one more title of Jesus that we must understand clearly. Jesus is the Lord. Why do we call him Lord? In the Old Testament Yahweh was God's name. To show reverence for this name, the word *Lord* was generally used in place of *Yahweh.* Lord, therefore, is a divine title reserved for God. And because Jesus is a divine Person and the Son of God, he, too, is called Lord. We see this often in the gospels, as in Luke 11:1, where Jesus' disciples said to him, "Lord, teach us to pray." Then he taught them the Lord's Prayer.

 Which of these titles of Jesus is especially meaningful to you? Tell why.

Scripture INSIGHT

The biblical authors did not divide their books into chapters and verses. They wrote a continuous manuscript without any divisions whatsoever. When, then, did we get chapters and verses in the Bible? It happened in A.D. 1226 when Stephen Langton, the archbishop of Canterbury in England, decided to divide each book into numbered chapters. Later, in 1551, a French printer named Robert Estienne divided these chapters into smaller segments called verses. These divisions made it easier to find one's way around the Bible.

The division into chapters and verses is universally followed today. It is very practical because everyone now knows where to find a passage, or section, of the Bible when the proper reference is given. For example, Mark 2:4 means the Gospel of Mark, chapter 2, verse 4. It can mean nothing else. And the use of numbered references makes it unnecessary for people to print out entire sections of the Bible.

Bible references can offer even more details. For example, Mark 2:1–12 means the Gospel of Mark, chapter 2, verses 1 through 12. This is the way we indicate the whole of Mark's account of the healing of the paralytic. Mark 2—4 is a different reference. The longer dash indicates that we move not just from verse to verse but from chapter to chapter. So Mark 2—4 means the Gospel of Mark, chapters 2 through 4.

The Lord's Prayer

In the gospels Jesus is frequently described as being at prayer, especially at important moments in his life. After his baptism by John the Baptist, Jesus went out to the desert to pray. Later he prayed before he called the twelve apostles to follow him. He prayed at his transfiguration and again in the garden of Gethsemane before his passion. He prayed alone; he prayed with others in the synagogue; he even prayed on the cross.

As Jesus went about his preaching, crowds of people pressed in upon him. That is one reason why he sometimes needed to go off by himself to a quiet place for prayer. On these occasions he would often pray throughout the whole night. What would Jesus do during these long times of prayer? He would be in silent communion with his Father, whom he often addressed as Abba.

Abba was an Aramaic word that expressed deep respect and affection for one's father. It was similar to our word *Dad* and showed how intimate Jesus was with the Father.

One time, Luke reports, the disciples saw Jesus at prayer; they realized how deeply he was in communion with the Father. They were so impressed that they wanted to be able to pray as Jesus was praying. So after he had finished his prayer, they said to Jesus, "Lord, teach us to pray" (Luke 11:1). Then Jesus taught them the prayer that we know today as the Our Father, or the Lord's Prayer. A short version of the prayer is found in Luke 11:2–4 and a long version in Matthew 6:9–13. The Church's liturgical tradition has followed Matthew's long version, which has seven petitions. Let's take a look at the prayer as we recite it today.

Our Father, who art in heaven We open the prayer by calling God our Father. We dare to do this because by Baptism into the death and resurrection of Jesus Christ, we are the adopted sons and daughters of God. Baptism makes us children of God. Jesus invited us to say, not *my* Father, but *our* Father, reminding us that we pray as baptized members of the Church community.

Hallowed be thy name In this first petition we proclaim that God alone is holy. Standing before the awesome mystery of God, we cry out using the words that come from the prophet Isaiah: "Holy, holy, holy" (Isaiah 6:3). This is what the word *hallowed* means: "holy." God, who is so completely different from anyone or anything that we know, always remains a mystery. But he has revealed himself to us and has done this most fully in Jesus.

Thy kingdom come To be part of God's kingdom means to be loved and protected by God. The kingdom of God is a symbol reminding everyone that God is the Lord of the universe, who takes care of his people and brings them salvation. The kingdom of God is God's rule and reign over people's lives. In this petition we pray that the kingdom will become a reality for all people.

Thy will be done on earth as it is in heaven This petition is connected to the first two. It reminds us that Jesus said, "Not everyone who says to me, 'Lord, Lord,' will enter the kingdom of heaven, but only the one who does the will of my Father in heaven" (Matthew 7:21). As children of God we have to be people who actively proclaim God's holiness and work for his kingdom.

Give us this day our daily bread Trusting in God as his children, we pray for our nourishment, both physical and spiritual. Only God can truly satisfy the hungers of the world. This petition reminds us that so many in the world go to bed hungry each night for lack of bread. So we must realize our responsibility to care for those less fortunate, who are victims of poverty and oppression. Because we are followers of Jesus, we pledge to work at changing any situation that supports injustice. This petition also reminds us of the Eucharist, the Bread of Life.

And forgive us our trespasses as we forgive those who trespass against us In this fifth petition we admit that we must forgive others if we hope to receive God's forgiveness. It is as simple as that.

And lead us not into temptation God does not tempt us, nor will God let us be tempted beyond our strength. We pray that we may always choose to do God's will, as the Holy Spirit guides and strengthens us.

But deliver us from evil Everyone has to struggle against evil. But we know that Jesus has saved us from sin. He sends the Holy Spirit, who brings us the grace to live in hope.

Choose one petition of the Our Father. Then write a prayer of your own, using that petition as your focus or theme. Share it with others.

CATHOLIC TEACHINGS

About the Lord's Prayer

The Church reminds us that the Our Father is the prayer Jesus himself gave to the Church. This prayer brings us into communion with God the Father and his Son, Jesus Christ. It has been described as the "most perfect of prayers," and the Church teaches that it is "truly the summary of the whole gospel" (*Catechism*, 2774).

PUTTING IT TOGETHER

things to think about

Which do you think is more difficult for people: to appreciate Jesus as divine or as human? Explain.

Why do you think Jesus spent so much time talking about his relationship with the Father?

things to share

Explain to someone why it is so important to understand the Old Testament in order to know Jesus Christ.

Share with someone that part of the Lord's Prayer that has the most meaning for you at this time in your life. Don't forget to tell why.

WORDS TO REMEMBER

Find and define the following:

Yahweh _____
_____
_____

Messiah_____
_____
_____

OnLine
WITH THE PARISH

The alpha and omega are often displayed on chalices and other sacred vessels. Sometimes these symbols are used on vestments, altar cloths and covers, prayer books, and hymnals. They may even appear in stained glass or other works of art. See whether the alpha and omega have been used in your parish church or neighboring parish churches. Explain to someone why these symbols are so important in our Catholic life.

What clues to his divinity did Jesus give to the people whom he encountered?

1

What is the significance of ending so many of our prayers with the words *through Christ our Lord*?

2

Why is the phrase *I AM* so important in John's Gospel?

3

What do we mean when we say that Jesus is the Messiah?

4

Why can we address the Father of Jesus as our Father, too?

5

Life in the Spirit

Now that you know so much more about the Lord's Prayer, use it as the focus of your prayer this week. Remember that we proclaim it at Baptism, at Confirmation, and at the Eucharist. Say each petition slowly and meaningfully. After each petition pause to reflect on its meaning in your life. As you complete the Lord's Prayer, let your amen be your yes to all that God has revealed to us in Jesus.

CHAPTER 9

The Power
and the Glory

For the kingdom, the power,
and the glory are yours,
now and for ever.

Have you ever heard someone say,
"It was a miracle that we won the game," or
"It was a miracle that I passed my exams"?
Have you ever called something a miracle?
What did you mean when you used this word?

Jesus the Miracle Worker

Have you ever noticed that many words with a religious meaning have passed into our everyday language? For example, someone may say to you that last night's sunset was "inspiring." You know from your study of the New Testament that using the word *inspiring* in this way misses the point. *Inspiration* is a technical word that refers to the influence of the Holy Spirit on a writer of the Bible. Other religious words that are often reduced to merely popular meanings include *revelation*, *incarnation*, *divine*, and *transcendence*.

Miracle is also one of these technical words. In everyday speech people use it to mean an unusual event of any type. In Catholic usage, however, a miracle means so much more. That is because this word is used most frequently when we refer to Jesus and his ministry in the New Testament.

The New Testament writers did not record the details of all the miracles worked by Jesus. The exact number is unknown, but there must have been a great many of them. We can say this because time and time again the gospels give summary statements about Jesus and his ministry. The following passage is a good example:

> When it was evening, after sunset, they brought to him all who were ill or possessed by demons. The whole town was gathered at the door. He cured many who were sick with various diseases, and he drove out many demons.
> Mark 1:32–34

A correct definition of miracle requires the context of faith. A miracle is a special act of God. When we claim that a miracle has taken place, we are saying that God has acted in a special way, in a way that goes beyond all human possibilities. We say that it is an extraordinary event caused by God's power.

How did Jesus perform these extraordinary works? Was he like a magician who used mysterious words such as *abracadabra*? No. Jesus was not a magician. Even though magic can be a wonderful show, it is not the work of God. The word *magic* in the technical sense is the human attempt to control the forces of the universe for one's own advantage. But magic is an illusion; it is not reality. It has nothing to do with faith and nothing to do with miracles. Magic is really the complete opposite of miracles. Miracles are never works of manipulation; they are always works of compassion and love. They are works of God.

We know that Jesus was filled with compassion and love. That is why the miracles he performed were such an important part of his ministry. The gospels are filled with specific miracle accounts that enable us to understand Jesus and his mission in the world. Besides the many general references to the miracle activity of Jesus, the gospels give the details of thirty-six different miracles worked by him. These miracles fall into four categories:

- healing miracles
- nature miracles
- exorcisms, or driving out of demons
- bringing the dead back to life.

In the lessons that follow, we will look at each of these miracle categories so that we, too, may profess our faith in the divine work of Jesus. Even more important, we will be able to feel the love and compassion that Jesus has for all people.

This New Testament passage and others like it describe Jesus as the worker of many miracles. This means that Jesus not only spoke with divine authority; he also acted with divine authority. He was a miracle worker. A *miracle* is an extraordinary event that is beyond human power and is brought about by God in the context, or setting, of faith.

Does this mean that people of faith think of Jesus as a type of superman with superhuman strength, X-ray vision, or the ability to fly? Absolutely not. Characters in comic books, movies, and television shows are pictured as doing unusual things; but such characters are imaginary, not real. They have nothing to do with our faith and nothing to do with the power of Jesus.

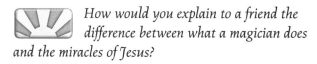 *How would you explain to a friend the difference between what a magician does and the miracles of Jesus?*

Miracle Accounts

Time and again Jesus reached out in love to touch those who were hurting. He did this because of his compassion for others and to give praise and glory to the Father. That is why his miracle activity was so important. Anyone reading the gospels for the first time notices how frequently miracles are mentioned. Take the Gospel of Mark, for example. It is only about 670 verses long. Yet 209 of those verses are about Jesus' miracles. That's over thirty percent of the gospel! Obviously miracles were important for Mark and the other gospel writers.

As we read the miracle accounts in the gospels, we notice that most of them are presented to us in a specific format. That is because the evangelists reported miracles to teach us important lessons about Jesus and our life of faith. The miracle accounts are written in a particular style that usually includes five points:

- an introduction telling who is involved in this miracle account and what is happening
- a request for Jesus' help that shows the faith of the person or people in need
- Jesus' response
- the result of Jesus' intervention
- a reaction of the spectators, such as fear or astonishment.

Of the thirty-six miracles reported in the gospels, many have these five points. Some do not. It depends on the details that an individual evangelist wants to give in a miracle narrative.

Miracles of Healing

The miracle accounts most frequently recorded in the gospels have to do with physical healing. It is easy to see why this is so because curing the sick was an important ministry for Jesus. Sickness and disease were especially frightening for people in biblical times. Remember, medicine was not yet scientifically advanced. There were no X rays, antibiotics, or vaccines. Sick people had few if any choices except to suffer. There were no hospitals, emergency rooms, or clinics. Even eyeglasses had not yet been invented. Terrible diseases that are treatable today, such as leprosy, meant certain and painful death. People even thought that such

sickness and disease might be the result of their own or their parents' sins. No wonder people were so afraid of illness.

In the midst of this suffering, Jesus came bringing healing and wholeness. One memorable healing miracle of Jesus was that of the centurion's servant. Let's take a closer look to see how it follows the format of the miracle accounts in the gospels.

In the introduction of this account, Jesus enters the town of Capernaum. There a Roman centurion comes before him to make a request. A *centurion* was a military officer in charge of one hundred men. This centurion had a favorite servant who was ill. That is why the centurion came to Jesus: to ask that the servant be cured. The centurion said to Jesus, "Lord, I am not worthy to have you enter under my roof; only say the word and my servant will be healed" (Matthew 8:8).

Because this centurion was a pagan, Jesus was amazed at his display of faith and said to the disciples, "Amen, I say to you, in no one in Israel have I found such faith" (Matthew 8:10). Then Jesus turned to the centurion and said, "You may go; as you have believed, let it be done for you" (Matthew 8:13). The result of this encounter with Jesus was the healing of the centurion's servant. The gospel account reports that the servant was healed at the very hour that Jesus spoke. Because the servant was cured far away from the spectators, no reaction could be reported. No doubt the reaction came later, especially among the members of the centurion's household.

This miracle, like all the miracles of Jesus, had nothing to do with magic. It was all about faith. It centered on a relationship of faith between a person and Jesus. The centurion did not hear Jesus mumble a magic formula. There were no puffs of smoke or flashes of light. The healing actually took place quietly and far away. Sometimes Jesus' miracles included a gesture, such as a touch. But Jesus never asked people to do something harmful or superstitious to make the miracle occur.

It is important to realize that Jesus did not look for opportunities to show off his power. He worked miracles almost hesitantly. When people came to him, Jesus often instructed those whom he cured not to tell anyone what had happened (Mark 1:44). Jesus even got angry with those who expected miracles as a proof of his power. Miracles were the sign that God's loving power was at work in the world in a wholly new way in Jesus.

 Look at the chart, and choose a favorite healing miracle story. In what ways is your faith in Jesus strengthened by hearing about this miracle?

Healing Miracles of Jesus

Miracle	Matthew	Mark	Luke	John
Cleansing of a leper	8:2	1:40	5:12	
Healing a centurion's servant	8:5		7:1	
Cure of Peter's mother-in-law	8:14	1:30	4:38	
Evening healings of the sick	8:16	1:32	4:40	
Healing of a paralytic	9:2	2:3	5:18	
Curing the hemorrhaging woman	9:20	5:25	8:43	
Healing two blind men	9:27			
Restoring a man's withered hand	12:9	3:1	6:6	
Giving sight to the blind	20:30	10:46	18:35	
Healing a deaf mute		7:31		
Healing a blind man at Bethsaida		8:22		
Cure of a crippled woman			13:11	
Healing the man with dropsy			14:1	
Cleansing ten lepers			17:11	
Restoring the ear of the high priest's servant			22:50	
Healing the royal official's son				4:46
Curing the infirm man at the Bethesda Pool				5:1
Healing the man born blind				9:1

Nature Miracles

Unlike miracles of healing, which deal directly with people, *nature miracles* deal directly with impersonal forces or objects. For example, Jesus calms a storm at sea or changes water into wine. Some people may be surprised to learn that the only miracle reported in all four gospel accounts is a nature miracle: the feeding of the five thousand. This miracle account is commonly called the multiplication of loaves and fishes.

Nature miracles are a part of the biblical tradition. They show God's activity in the world and are described in both the Old and the New Testaments.

In the Old Testament During the exodus, when Moses led the Israelites out of slavery in Egypt, many nature miracles occurred. Among these miraculous events were the ten plagues (Exodus 7:14—11:10). Moses had gone to the pharaoh to demand the people's freedom, but the pharaoh stubbornly refused. Only when God's almighty power was demonstrated in the ten plagues did the pharaoh give up and let the people go free to return to the promised land.

God also demonstrated miraculous power when the Israelites crossed the Red Sea and again when they wandered in the desert. He gave the people manna, a food to sustain them on their journey. It is called "bread from heaven" in Exodus 16:4. On another occasion the sun is said to have stood still at the word of Joshua (Joshua 10:12–13).

Later on the prophets Elijah and Elisha were God's instruments in working great wonders for the people (1 Kings 17—2 Kings 13). With God's power Elijah defeated the pagan priests of Baal (1 Kings 18). Elisha supported a poor widow by a miraculous multiplication of oil (2 Kings 4). He even multiplied barley loaves so that one hundred men could eat (2 Kings 4:42). All these miracles were great signs and wonders showing forth God's power and his personal concern for his people.

In the New Testament Was Jesus a miracle worker just like Elijah and Elisha in the Old Testament? No. Jesus was different. He was the Son of God, and therefore he worked miracles on his own authority. Elijah and Elisha did not work miracles on their own authority; it was God's power working through them. But there was a parallel between the nature miracles of the Old Testament and those of the New Testament.

Think for a moment about the nature miracles of Jesus. Just as God parted the waters of the sea so that the Israelites could escape pharaoh's army, Jesus calmed the storm at sea and even walked on the water. Just as God gave his people manna in the desert, Jesus fed the hungry people with only a few loaves and fishes. Just as God had brought order into the world at creation, now Jesus was bringing order and salvation into the world. All the miracles of Jesus showed that God was now bringing to fulfillment in Jesus what had already begun in the Old Testament.

One of the most spectacular of Jesus' recorded miracles was his walking on the water. In the account Jesus has gone off by himself to pray and has sent his disciples on ahead of him to cross the Sea of Galilee. Alone at night on the water, the disciples are tossed about by strong wind. Suddenly they see Jesus walking toward them on the water! Thinking that they are seeing a ghost, the disciples are filled with fear. Jesus comes toward them, identifies himself, and gets into the boat. Immediately the storm is calmed, and all are safe.

This Jesus who walks on the water is the same one who reaches out to others in need of healing. This is the same Jesus who has joined with his friends and with families at wedding celebrations and other festivities. But this is also the Jesus who is so different from us, full of divine power not just over illness but over all creation itself.

Think of the miracle of Jesus calming a storm at sea. After he did this, his disciples were filled with amazement and said to one another, "What sort of man is this, whom even the winds and the sea obey?" (Matthew 8:27). All the miracles of Jesus help us to answer that question. He truly is the Son of God, who does great wonders by his own authority. He performed miracles, not as a showy display of power, but as invitations to faith. Jesus' miracles are still invitations to faith today.

Two terms are used in the New Testament to describe a miracle: *sign* and *power*. Miracles are signs that God is at work. They are deeds of divine power that stir the hearts of people to wonder and awe. Miracles are not isolated displays of God's power over the laws of nature. Rather they are works of God that show his loving care and plan of salvation for the world.

Study the chart, and decide which of Jesus' nature miracles is most meaningful to you. Tell why.

Scripture INSIGHT

We know how important John the Baptist was at the time of Jesus, but John never worked miracles. He was a great preacher and had a great following of disciples, but Jesus was the miracle worker.

Nature Miracles of Jesus

Miracle	Matthew	Mark	Luke	John
Calming a storm at sea	8:23	4:35	8:22	
Feeding the five thousand	14:13	6:30	9:10	6:1
Walking on the water	14:25	6:45		6:16
Feeding the four thousand	15:32	8:1		
The coin for the Temple tax	17:24			
Cursing the fig tree	21:18	11:12		
A miraculous catch of fish			5:1	
Changing water into wine				2:1
A second miraculous catch of fish				21:1

Other Miracles

Each time we pray the Lord's Prayer, we ask God to deliver us from evil. At each Mass, just before we share a sign of peace, we also ask God to deliver us from every evil and from all anxiety. Why do we do this? As human beings we naturally fear sickness and disease. We can be terrified by the forces of nature unleashed in a hurricane, flood, or tornado. We also fear the evil that all too often is part of the world around us: violence, homelessness, murder, greed, hunger, and war. Perhaps our greatest fear of all is death. How are we as Catholics to face these fears?

We have already seen how Jesus dealt with physical illness and the forces of nature. But there are other miracle accounts that show us how Jesus dealt with the presence of evil in the world and with death.

Driving Out Demons The New Testament records that Jesus drove out devils, or evil spirits, on many different occasions. As the chart makes clear, six specific accounts of this type of miracle are narrated in the gospels. The technical term for the driving out of demons, or devils, is *exorcism,* a word meaning "to command to go out." In Jesus' ministry of announcing the good news, he sometimes encountered people who were possessed by evil spirits. These were extraordinary circumstances, and the people who were possessed by demons suffered greatly. Jesus was not afraid to confront evil because he knew that evil could never overcome him.

One day Jesus drove a demon out of a man. When the Pharisees saw this, they accused Jesus of exorcising demons by the power of Satan. Jesus told the Pharisees, "Every kingdom divided against itself will be laid waste, and no town or house divided against itself will stand. And if Satan drives out Satan, he is divided against himself" (Matthew 12:25–26). Jesus was saying that it takes a power greater than Satan's to defeat demons. That power is the power of Jesus. The coming of God's kingdom in Jesus meant the defeat of Satan. The miracles worked by Jesus showed that the Father had sent him for our salvation.

The Pharisees opposed Jesus on many other occasions because he seemed to be going against everything that was important to them. After all, the *Pharisees* were an influential group of Jews who emphasized careful observance of the traditions and laws of their religion. It is no wonder that the Pharisees, seeing what Jesus was doing, were often at odds with him. He exercised divine power in driving out demons. He forgave sins. He claimed to be able to do what the Pharisees knew only God could do.

Another group, the Sadducees, also opposed Jesus at times. The *Sadducees* were influential members of priestly families in Israel who did not appreciate the interpretations of the law given by the Pharisees. However, the gospels describe them as often joining the Pharisees in criticizing Jesus.

Raising the Dead For many people Jesus' most dramatic miracles are the ones in which he raised people from the dead. As the chart makes clear, there are three such accounts in the gospels. These reports are about people who were actually dead. Lazarus, the friend of Jesus, had already been dead for several days, and his body had begun to decay.

Each of the individuals whom Jesus raised from the dead was brought back to continue living a normal life. They were brought back not just for a visit but to take up their earthly lives again. At some later date they would experience death again as part of the normal course of human existence.

Whenever we hear the miracle accounts of Jesus being proclaimed, what should we as people of faith think about them? We should recall that Jesus' miracles are works that do more than help us to identify him as a divine Person, the Son of God. They also confirm all that Jesus revealed to us. They are special signs of God's love and mercy that come to us in Jesus.

The miracles give witness to things that we cannot see, to the power that Jesus has not only to cure the body but also to bring real spiritual healing. Jesus' miracles are a sign of his work for our salvation. They are also signs of his work down through the centuries. The miraculous catch of fish, for example, is a sign of the future ministry of Christ's Church in its work of evangelizing the whole world. Likewise, the multiplication of loaves and fishes points to the Eucharist and to Jesus' unlimited power to take care of our deepest needs and hungers. It is no wonder that the gospels spend so much time reporting his miracles.

Review the chart of Jesus' exorcisms and raisings from the dead. Do you have a favorite among these miracle accounts? Explain.

CATHOLIC TEACHINGS

About Miracles

Can miracles happen today? The Church recognizes that God can perform a miracle at any time. But God always does this within the context of faith, grace, and salvation and never for show or display. The Church does not conclude that a miracle has taken place just because something cannot be easily explained. The Church rigorously investigates any claims of miraculous happenings, such as those that occur at the famous shrine of Lourdes in France. Every possible natural explanation must first be tried and rejected before a miracle can be claimed.

Exorcisms by Jesus

Miracle	Matthew	Mark	Luke	John
Casting demons into a herd of swine	8:28	5:1	8:26	
Driving a demon from a mute man	9:32			
Curing the blind and mute demoniac	12:22		11:14	
Freeing the daughter of the Canaanite woman	15:21	7:24		
Healing the boy possessed by a demon	17:14	9:17	9:38	
Casting out an unclean spirit		1:23	4:33	

Jesus Raising the Dead

Miracle	Matthew	Mark	Luke	John
Raising the daughter of Jairus	9:18, 23	5:22, 35	8:40, 49	
Raising the widow's son at the city of Nain			7:11	
The raising of Lazarus				11:43

things
to think about

Now that you have finished this study of Jesus' miracle activity, how has your understanding of miracles changed? Explain.

Why do you think that faith is so important in understanding Jesus' miracles?

things
to share

In what ways are the miracles of Jesus so different from the activities of magicians?

The next time you hear people say that it will be a miracle if they pass their exams or win a game, what will you say as a person of faith?

WORDS TO REMEMBER

Find and define the following:

miracle _____
_____
_____

exorcism _____
_____
_____

OnLine
WITH THE PARISH

Sometimes parishes sponsor pilgrimages to shrines such as Lourdes in France. Both the sick and those who help the sick make these journeys. Take a moment to pray for the sick and suffering members of your parish and those who minister to them.

Name the four categories of the miracles of Jesus.

1

What are the usual five points that are part of a miracle account in the New Testament?

2

Explain the difference between nature miracles and healing miracles.

3

Who were the Pharisees, and why did they oppose Jesus' exorcisms?

4

What do the miracles of Jesus tell us about his identity?

5

Life
in the Spirit

The centurion in the gospel had great faith and trust in Jesus. Make his prayer, which has become part of our eucharistic celebration, one of your daily prayers:

Lord, I am not worthy to receive you,
but only say the word and I shall be healed.

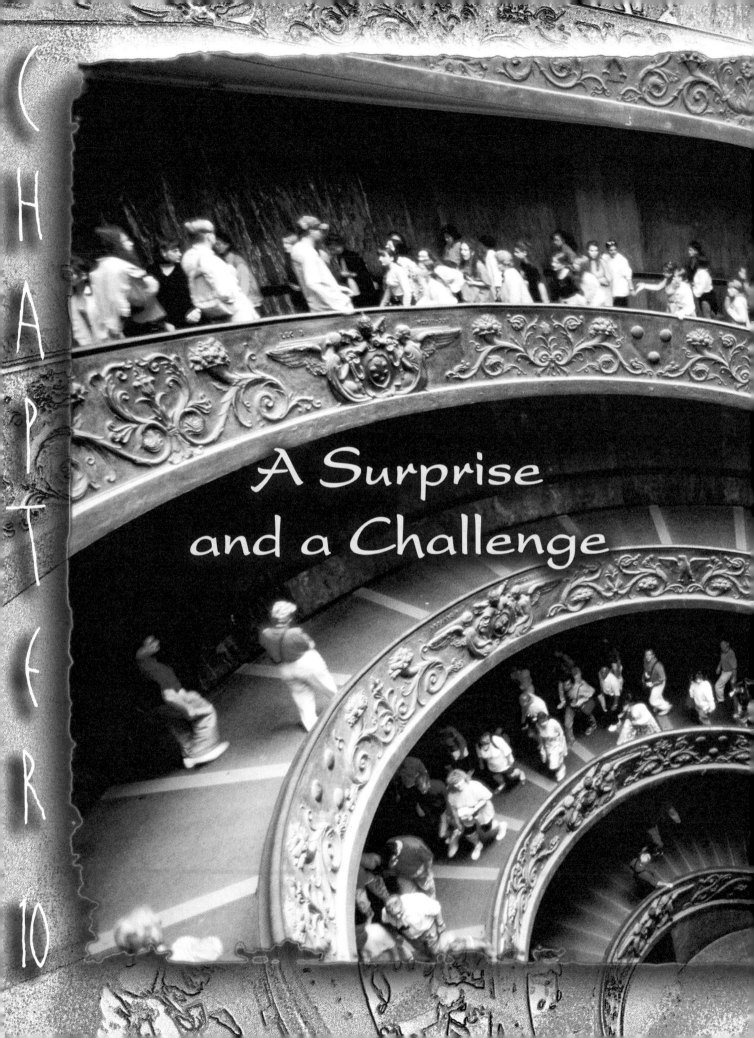

A Surprise
and a Challenge

Everyone who listens to these words of mine and acts on them will be like a wise man who built his house on rock.

Matthew 7:24

What do you think makes a person a great teacher?

Jesus the Teacher

Jesus must have been an outstanding teacher, for the gospels record that crowds of people pressed in upon him to hear him speak. One time the number was so great that Jesus had to get into a boat to teach the huge crowd standing along the shoreline (Matthew 13:2). Wherever people were—at the seashore or along the road, in a synagogue or at the Temple, in the marketplace or in a private home—there was Jesus, telling them about God's love and mercy. Jesus' message and way of teaching were powerful because he left the people astonished (Luke 4:32). His words touched their hearts and changed their lives.

The message that he brought was an urgent one because it concerned people's eternal salvation. Jesus told the people about God's love, but he also challenged them to change their lives and to turn once again to God. This was the message that he shared with people as he traveled the countryside. This was the same message he wanted his followers to share as he sent them out among the people.

How did Jesus teach? One of the characteristics of his teaching was that he spoke in colorful and picturesque language. Using examples from everyday life, he compared his followers to the salt of the earth and the light of the world. Very often, but not always, he taught in parables. A *parable* is a fictitious short story that uses ordinary experiences of life to teach a deeper spiritual lesson. So if we want to understand Jesus and his teaching more fully, we must look closely at his use of parables.

What goes into making a parable? There are four basic ingredients: A parable is built on similes, is true to life, is filled with surprises, and is told to present a challenge.

Built on Similes You already know from your study of English that a simile is a figure of speech used to get a point across. A simile does this by comparing two different things. The word *like* is often, but not always, used in making the comparison. Perhaps you have heard people say that someone "looks like a scared rabbit." That expression contains a simile.

Jesus also used similes when he taught. For example, he once told his disciples, "I am sending you like lambs among wolves" (Luke 10:3). When he taught in parables, Jesus often began with a comparison. He might start with the phrase "The kingdom of heaven is like" and then compare the kingdom to a tiny mustard seed planted in a field or to a buried treasure (Matthew 13:31, 44).

True to Life Where did Jesus get his ideas for parables? The answer is simple: from everyday life. He spoke about things that everyone knew from experience. When he talked about the countryside, he spoke about stone fences and thorns. When he talked about shepherding, he spoke of sheep and wolves. When he talked about farming, he spoke about seeds and the harvest. When he talked about the marketplace, he spoke of workers and wineskins. He also spoke about the relationship between children and their parents. No wonder people were attracted to Jesus the teacher! They could see everything he talked about and relate it to their lives.

In what ways does this photo suggest that parables are filled with surprises?

Filled with Surprises Good storytellers generally surprise their audiences with unusual twists and turns in their stories. They do this to keep the attention of their listeners and to keep them alert. Jesus was such a storyteller. He made his listeners sit up and take notice. Think how the vivid parable of the Good Samaritan (Luke 10:29–37) caught people off guard. In the cast of three characters—the priest, the Levite, and the hated Samaritan—who would have thought that the hero of the story would be the Samaritan, a foreigner? Certainly none of Jesus' listeners.

Presents a Challenge Jesus did not use parables just to entertain people. He wanted to challenge them in the way they thought about God and lived their lives. Today the parables bring us the same message and challenge of Jesus. For the sake of convenience, we will divide the parables of Jesus into three groups in this chapter: parables about the kingdom, parables about God's grace, and parables about judgment. All the parables teach us about God's love and care for us. They illustrate for us God's mercy. They remind us that we are responsible for one another and that we are to be faithful members of God's kingdom. They sometimes make us feel uncomfortable because they speak about our accountability before God.

What everyday experiences from our own time and place do you think Jesus might use to tell one of his parables today? How would he challenge us?

The Kingdom

Today there are many types of leaders of nations. Some are presidents who have been elected by the people. Others are kings or queens who inherit their thrones because they are members of a royal family. In Jesus' time the leader of a country was usually a king. A good king was to be like the father of his nation. For Israel, David was the ideal king. He cared for his people, protected them from danger, and guaranteed that justice was carried out throughout his kingdom.

According to Mark's Gospel, Jesus began his public ministry by proclaiming, "The kingdom of God is at hand. Repent, and believe in the gospel" (Mark 1:15). The kingdom of God, or the kingdom of heaven as it is called by Matthew, was an important part of Jesus' teaching. Many of the parables in the synoptic gospels are about that kingdom. Since we are the disciples of Jesus and are called to build up God's kingdom, we must have a clear understanding of that kingdom.

Jesus said, "My kingdom does not belong to this world" (John 18:36). If the kingdom of God was not a place, what did Jesus mean? What did his followers understand when he preached about the kingdom? The idea of God as king is a theme that is found in the Old Testament. Here are some examples:

- Yahweh is king of Israel: "The LORD your God is your king" (1 Samuel 12:12).
- Yahweh is king of all nations: "The LORD is king; let the earth rejoice" (Psalm 97:1).
- Yahweh is king of all creation: "The LORD is king, robed with majesty" (Psalm 93:1).

The idea of God as king was therefore familiar to Jesus and the people of his time. To be part of God's kingdom meant to be loved and protected by God. No wonder Jesus spoke so often about it! The *kingdom of God* is a symbol reminding everyone that God is the Lord of the universe, who cares for his people and brings them salvation. Members of God's kingdom are to return God's love and follow God's law. God must have a central place in their lives.

The kingdom of God is not a place. It is God's rule and reign over people's lives. Jesus wanted everyone to know that they would find the kingdom of God in him. Pointing to himself, he said, "Behold, the kingdom of God is among you" (Luke 17:21). God's kingdom, then, is found in Jesus. How did Jesus use parables to teach people about the kingdom?

In one parable Jesus said the kingdom was like a tiny mustard seed. People are surprised to discover just how small a mustard seed is. Yet, when it is planted and nourished, it grows into a huge bush, and "birds of the sky come and dwell in its branches" (Matthew 13:32). By teaching about the kingdom in this way, Jesus was telling us that the kingdom of God is not yet complete. It came in a dramatic way in Jesus himself, but the kingdom still needs to grow and to be nourished by us, Jesus' disciples. We have to take an active part in making that kingdom grow. That is why we pray "thy kingdom come."

The parables also remind us that we must be alert to the presence of God's kingdom and be ready to accept God's invitation to be part of it. The parable of the wedding feast (Matthew 22:1–14) makes this clear. We did not choose God's kingdom; rather, God chose us to be part of it. We are called to respond to that invitation.

Jesus was so excited about the good news of the kingdom that he wanted everyone to know about it. So he gathered around himself a community of disciples, the Church. He did this so that we could proclaim the good news of the kingdom and work for its completion. The Church and the kingdom of God are closely connected. Catholics believe that the Church is "on earth the seed and beginning of that kingdom" (*Catechism*, 541).

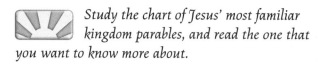

Study the chart of Jesus' most familiar kingdom parables, and read the one that you want to know more about.

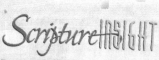

It is interesting to see that some details in the parables differ among the synoptics. Choose a kingdom parable that appears in more than one gospel, and compare the versions to see how many details are different.

Familiar Parables About the Kingdom

Parable	Matthew	Mark	Luke
The sower	13:1–23	4:1–20	8:4–15
The weeds among the wheat	13:24–30		
The mustard seed	13:31–32	4:30–32	13:18–19
The buried treasure and the pearls	13:44–46		
The net	13:47–50		
The unforgiving servant	18:23–35		
The great feast			14:15–24
The Pharisee and the tax collector			18:9–14
The workers in the vineyard	20:1–16		
The tenants	21:33–46	12:1–12	20:9–19
The wedding feast	22:1–14		
The ten virgins	25:1–13		

Knowing God's Love

Jesus loved everyone, but he had a special place in his heart for sinners. He never hesitated to talk with them and even went to their homes. Some people criticized him for this and said, "This man welcomes sinners and eats with them" (Luke 15:2). Jesus did not just eat with sinners; he sought them out to bring them the good news of God's mercy.

To those who were shocked by his love of sinners, Jesus told a parable. We call it the parable of the lost sheep. Jesus said:

> What man among you having a hundred sheep and losing one of them would not leave the ninety-nine in the desert and go after the lost one until he finds it? And when he does find it, he sets it on his shoulders with great joy and, upon his arrival home, he calls together his friends and neighbors and says to them, "Rejoice with me because I have found my lost sheep." I tell you, in just the same way there will be more joy in heaven over one sinner who repents than over ninety-nine righteous people who have no need of repentance.
> Luke 15:4–7

What a beautiful example of the way Jesus taught! This moving story includes all four ingredients of a parable:

- Jesus likens the experience of God's mercy and forgiveness to a shepherd who seeks after a lost sheep. Even though Jesus does not use the word *like,* he is still making a comparison.

- Jesus is talking not about something make-believe but about something that is true to life. Everyone knows what a shepherd is and what sheep are and that sheep tend to wander.

- The surprise of the story is that the shepherd would leave ninety-nine sheep alone and unprotected to go after one sheep. The first reaction of Jesus' listeners to this story would have been that this shepherd was foolish. He was taking a chance that the other sheep might wander away while he was looking for the one lost sheep. That did not make good business sense. Imagine how this made Jesus' audience alert for the rest of the story.

- One challenge of this story is to place our lives in God's care. We should never fear to do so because we know that he is actively seeking out sinners to forgive them.

Parables of Grace

Just as we looked closely at the parable of the lost sheep, we can take all the parables about God's grace and look at them in the same way. In doing so, we will be reminded of many truths of our faith and have a deeper understanding of them. These truths include:

God Our Father These parables remind us in a dramatic way that God is our Father, who loves and cares for us. Catholics have a special term for the overwhelming love and care of God; it is God's providence. *God's providence* is his personal concern for each of his creatures.

Children of God As baptized members of the Church, we are the adopted sons and daughters of God in Jesus, the only Son of God. He is a divine Person. Through the grace of Baptism, we have become the adopted children of God and the brothers and sisters of Jesus. This can never be changed and is the reason we call God our Father.

God's Initiative God always takes the initiative, the first step, in seeking us out. We have not chosen God; God has chosen us. How wonderfully Jesus describes God's initiative in the parables of the lost sheep, the lost son, and the Good Samaritan. He

shares his own life with us. We call this sanctifying grace. *Sanctifying grace* is a participation in the very life of God that brings us into an intimate and permanent relationship with the Blessed Trinity. We first receive this divine gift at Baptism.

Our Response The next step in our relationship with God is our response. God never forces his love or his life upon anyone. We are free to reject it as the young man did in the parable of the lost son. But when we take that next step, God always surprises us with the generosity of his love. That is what it feels like to know God's love. It is always there for us.

These parables of grace can teach us valuable lessons each and every time we read them or hear them proclaimed. Each time we encounter the parables, we should place ourselves in them as one of the characters to learn once again the power of God's grace in our lives.

Which of the parables in the chart do you think young people need to hear the most today and why?

Familiar Parables About God's Grace

Parable	Matthew	Mark	Luke
The Good Samaritan			10:29–37
The lost sheep	18:12–14		15:4–7
The lost coin			15:8–10
The lost (prodigal) son			15:11–32
The persistent widow			18:1–8

Responsibility and Judgment

The gospels are filled not only with words of tenderness and love but also with words that challenge us. Jesus taught that people are accountable for their actions and that they must be sincere in what they do. Once he said to his disciples, "Why do you call me, 'Lord, Lord,' but not do what I command?" (Luke 6:46). He was telling people that to be his followers means more than simply talking about it. It requires action.

Sometimes we would rather not be reminded of our responsibilities. But the truth remains: The things that we do or do not do have consequences. At the end of our lives, God will judge us. At that judgment the good will be rewarded, and the bad will be punished. After all, we are made in God's image and should know the difference between good and evil. We also have the power to choose between the two.

To help people understand their responsibilities, Jesus told the parable of the talents, found in Matthew 25:14–30. A talent was a coin of great value. In this parable three servants are given different amounts of money by their master, who is going away on a trip. One is given five talents, another is given two talents, and the last is given one talent. When the master returns, he finds that the first two servants have doubled their talents. But out of fear the last servant buried the money and did nothing with it. The first two servants are praised by their master. The last is condemned and thrown out into the darkness.

The parable of the talents makes an important point: We are responsible for all the gifts we have been given by God. This means that we will be rewarded or punished according to our actions and the way we used our gifts. This point is made even clearer in the gospel verses that follow the parable of the talents. In Matthew 25:31–46 Jesus speaks about the end of the world, when he will come as the great judge accompanied by angels for the last judgment. At the *last judgment* everyone who ever lived will be present together. Then all of us will know where we stand in relation to one another and to Christ.

During the last judgment Jesus will separate the good from the bad, just as a "shepherd separates the sheep from the goats." He will judge us on the way we have treated "the least ones," those who are hungry, thirsty, strangers, naked, sick, imprisoned —all those whom Jesus identifies with himself. Those whom he has placed on his right will enjoy "eternal life." Those on his left will go off to "eternal punishment."

The eternal life that the good will enjoy is called heaven. *Heaven* is life forever with the Blessed Trinity. It is the state of supreme happiness in which those who have been faithful to God and his commandments will enjoy the beatific vision: seeing God "face-to-face." Those in hell, on the other hand, will be miserable for all eternity. *Hell* is eternal separation from God. It is the just punishment for those who have rejected God.

Jesus' teaching was meant, not to frighten us, but to remind us that the choice is ours. We can choose between living for heaven or living for hell. That choice will be made known before the whole world on the last day, the day of judgment.

Familiar Parables About Judgment

Parable	Matthew	Mark	Luke
The two foundations	7:24–27		
The rich fool			12:16–21
The dishonest steward			16:1–13
The rich man and Lazarus			16:19–31
The faithful servant	24:45–51		
The talents	25:14–30		
The ten gold coins			19:11–27

A Teacher with Authority

When Jesus taught about our responsibilities, the end of the world, and the last judgment, he taught as the Son of God. He spoke on his own authority and did not quote other rabbis or other teachers. Sometimes he would refer to the law of the Old Testament. He knew the heart of that law and felt free to interpret it in his own way. Jesus could do this because he was divine. For example, during the Sermon on the Mount, Jesus told the people, "You have heard that it was said, 'You shall love your neighbor and hate your enemy.' But I say to you, love your enemies, and pray for those who persecute you" (Matthew 5:43–44).

In reality the greatest teaching that Jesus did was to give us the example of his life. He came to serve others, not to be served. He came to lay down his life for others. He wanted us to love one another as he loved us. The proof of his love came most dramatically at the end of his life with his passion, death, and resurrection. That is where we now turn in our study of the New Testament.

Now that you are more familiar with the parables of Jesus, identify and explain the parable depicted on the cover of this textbook.

CATHOLIC TEACHINGS

About the Last Things

The Church teaches us that besides the last judgment, there is a particular judgment that will take place on the day of death. On that day Christ will judge the choice each individual has made and will determine the eternal reward or punishment that each deserves.

The Church also teaches us about purgatory. *Purgatory* is a process of final purification after death, in which those who have died in the state of grace grow in the holiness they need to enter heaven. The souls in purgatory are certain of heaven. We can help them by our good works and prayers, especially the Mass.

things to think about

Why do you think the parables of Jesus are so easy to remember?

Why was the *kingdom of God* a good symbol for Jesus to use to teach that God cares for his people and brings them salvation?

things to share

Tell what aspect of parables— for example, the surprise twist—interests you the most and why.

If someone said that it is difficult to know what Jesus wants his disciples to do, how would you respond? What evidence would you give to show that you know what Jesus wants of us?

WORDS TO REMEMBER

Find and define the following:

parable _____
_____
_____

last judgment _____
_____
_____

OnLine

WITH THE PARISH

Take one of Jesus' longer parables, such as the lost son or the Good Samaritan, and act it out with your group. You may want to put the parable into a modern setting and share it with young people or a group of senior citizens.

1. Explain how a parable is built on similes and is true to life.

2. Explain how a parable is filled with surprises and presents a challenge.

3. What do we mean by the providence of God?

4. Why can we call ourselves children of God?

5. Why did Jesus tell the parable of the talents?

Life in the Spirit

How wonderful it is to realize more and more each day how much God loves us and seeks us out. Think for a moment about Jesus' parable of the lost sheep. Picture a moment when you have felt lost or alone. Now quietly pray the words that begin Psalm 23:

The LORD is my shepherd;
there is nothing I lack.

The New and Everlasting Covenant

The Son of Man has come to seek
and to save what was lost.

Luke 19:10

Crucifixion in Blue (Composition II), Abraham Rattner, 1953

*O*ne day two Catholics were discussing which season
of the Church year was most important.
One said the Christmas season; the other said
the Easter Triduum. Which person do you think
was correct, and why?

The Greatest Events

The correct answer to the question must be the Easter Triduum. Why? Because the Triduum celebrates the greatest events of our salvation. The Triduum is the solemn three-day period that begins with the Evening Mass of the Lord's Supper on Holy Thursday and closes with evening prayer on Easter Sunday. Each "day" of the Triduum goes from evening to evening: Thursday evening to Friday evening, Friday evening to Saturday evening, and Saturday evening to Sunday evening.

Why are these three days so important and solemn? Why is the Triduum, rather than Christmas, the highest point of the liturgical year? Christmas is the celebration of the incarnation, but the very reason the incarnation took place was for our redemption. The Triduum commemorates the redeeming work of Jesus through his passion, death, and resurrection. Speaking of himself, Jesus said, "The Son of Man did not come to be served but to serve and to give his life as a ransom for many" (Mark 10:45).

In this quotation Jesus calls himself the Son of Man. It is an important title for him in the New Testament. Surprisingly this title is used only by Jesus when speaking of himself; it is not used for anyone else in the New Testament. We know that this title had several different meanings in the Old Testament and in popular Jewish literature at the time of Jesus. *Son of Man* also has several different meanings in the gospels. Jesus used the title in the following ways:

- referring to his human life (Luke 9:58)
- claiming divine powers (Mark 2:10)
- describing his mission (Luke 19:10)
- referring to his passion and death (Mark 10:45)
- describing himself coming on the clouds of heaven as judge (Matthew 24:30–31).

Whenever Jesus uses the title for himself, we have to look closely to see which meaning he had in mind. For example, in Mark 10:45 when Jesus speaks about the Son of Man coming as a ransom, he is talking about his own passion (suffering) and death as the Savior of the world. He is talking about the paschal mystery.

Paschal Mystery

The term *paschal mystery* refers to the passion, death, resurrection, and ascension of Jesus Christ. These are the important events of our redemption. Through these events Jesus our redeemer brought salvation to the whole world. He redeemed the human race and saved us from sin. He offered his life in sacrifice so that we might be reconciled to God. That is why John the Baptist said of Jesus, "Behold, the Lamb of God, who takes away the sin of the world" (John 1:29).

Why did John the Baptist refer to Jesus as a lamb? Because Jesus was the new paschal lamb. Just as an innocent lamb was sacrificed at the Passover celebration, so Jesus would be a sacrificial victim; he would be the Lamb of God. Even though he was sinless and did not deserve to suffer and die, Jesus offered his life on the cross so that we might be free from sin.

The paschal mystery did not end with Jesus' passion and death, however. Jesus conquered death and rose again. He also ascended into heaven and returned to the Father. It is no wonder, then, that the paschal mystery is so central to the Christian life. Not only does it recall the old covenant that God made with our ancestors in faith. It also reminds us of the new covenant that was made in the Blood of Jesus.

In the following three lessons, we will take a closer look at the deeper aspects of the paschal mystery as they are presented to us in the New Testament. How will we do this? We will use what we know about the Triduum as the framework to help guide our investigation. In this way we hope to come to a greater appreciation of what the Son of Man did for the world.

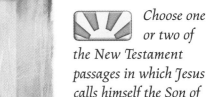

Choose one or two of the New Testament passages in which Jesus calls himself the Son of Man. Try to learn these passages by heart so that you will have a better understanding of Jesus and his mission.

129

Jesus Washing Peter's Feet, Ford Madox Brown, 19th century

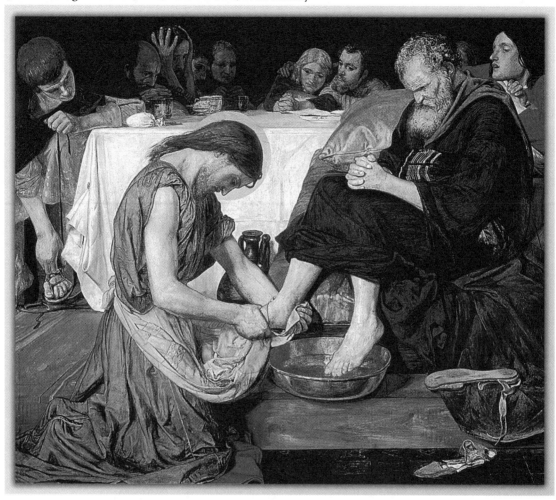

The Triduum Begins

A few days before he was to undergo his passion and death, Jesus made his way to Jerusalem for the Passover celebration. Events were about to unfold that would make this his last Passover. It must have been an emotional moment for him. Luke wrote that as Jesus drew near Jerusalem "he saw the city and wept over it" (Luke 19:41). Why did Jesus do this? One reason was that he knew he would be betrayed in Jerusalem by one of his apostles. Even though he had done so much for people, Jesus would be rejected in Jerusalem just as so many great prophets had been before him. How sad also for the gospel writers, who knew that Jerusalem itself had been destroyed in A.D. 70.

The gospels recall that when Jesus first entered Jerusalem, he was given a warm welcome. People waved palm branches and sang his praises, saying:

Blessed is the king who comes in the name of the Lord. Peace in heaven and glory in the highest.
Luke 19:38

 Do any of these words remind you of the prayers of the Mass? Which ones?

130

Like all faithful Jews, Jesus and his apostles prepared to celebrate the Passover. They gathered in Jerusalem to remember all that God had done for his people in delivering them from slavery in Egypt. This passing over from slavery to freedom was memorialized in a special meal that had been celebrated for many centuries. For Jesus this Passover meal would be the Last Supper he shared with his apostles. It would be a supper unlike any other. Why? Because in a wonderful way Jesus was about to teach the apostles of his love and give them a gift to last for all time.

A Lesson in True Love

During the Last Supper Jesus gave a beautiful lesson of love that his apostles would remember for all time. "Fully aware that the Father had put everything into his power and that he [Jesus] had come from God and was returning to God, he rose from supper and took off his outer garments. He took a towel and tied it around his waist. Then he poured water into a basin and began to wash the disciples' feet" (John 13:3–5).

Astonishing! The Lord of heaven and earth was bending over and washing the dusty feet of his apostles. This was the one who had so often spoken about coming to serve, not to be served. Now he was giving an example of service and love to those closest to him. Jesus said, "I have given you a model to follow, so that as I have done for you, you should also do" (John 13:15).

Earlier in his ministry Jesus had also addressed the theme of love. One day a Pharisee wanted to test Jesus and asked him which commandment was the greatest. Jesus reminded him of the teaching found in the Old Testament. Quoting Deuteronomy 6:5 and Leviticus 19:18, Jesus said that the greatest commandments were to love God with your whole being and to love your neighbor as yourself (Matthew 22:37–40).

Jesus was not abolishing the Ten Commandments or any part of God's law. But Jesus was inviting people to rediscover this law through him. The foundation of God's law was love of God and of neighbor. Jesus not only revealed who God is but also defined forever who one's neighbor is. In the parable of the Good Samaritan, he taught that a neighbor was no longer just a fellow Jew. For a follower of Jesus, one's neighbor includes every person in the world.

Later at the Last Supper, after Jesus washed the feet of his disciples, he summarized all his teaching on love and gave his disciples a *new commandment:* "Love one another. As I have loved you, so you also should love one another. This is how all will know that you are my disciples, if you have love for one another" (John 13:34–35). With this new commandment, Jesus was again putting himself on a par with his Father. Just as God had given the commandments to Moses, so now Jesus was giving a *new* commandment to his followers.

Love is still the hallmark of those who follow Jesus Christ. We are reminded of this in a dramatic way during the Evening Mass of the Lord's Supper on Holy Thursday. Before the Liturgy of the Eucharist begins, twelve members of the congregation are led to a special place in the church. The priest removes his chasuble and then, following the example of Jesus, he washes and dries the feet of each of the twelve. Each year as this ceremony is repeated, we witness once again a marvelous symbol of Christ's new commandment.

CATHOLIC ID For many years a beautiful song has been sung by Catholics during the Evening Mass of the Lord's Supper. In Latin the song is called "Ubi Caritas." The first line of the song is: "Where charity and love abide, there God is found."

The Triduum Continues

At the Last Supper Jesus did more than teach his apostles the truth about love and wash their feet. He shared a special meal with them. During the course of the meal, he took unleavened bread, gave thanks, broke it, and gave it to them, saying, "Take and eat; this is my body." Then he took a cup filled with wine. After giving thanks, he offered the cup to them, saying, "Drink from it, all of you, for this is my blood of the covenant, which will be shed on behalf of many for the forgiveness of sins" (Matthew 26:26–28).

With these actions and words, what had Jesus done? He had taken the Passover meal and transformed it from a simple meal commemorating a past event to a sacrificial meal sealing the new covenant in his Blood. This new covenant that God was making with his people would not be sealed in the blood of sacrificial animals. It would be sealed in the Blood of his only Son. From that moment, whenever the disciples of Jesus would gather together, they would remember what he had done at this Last Supper. At Jesus' command they would continue to break bread and share the cup of the new and everlasting covenant.

Catholics believe that what Jesus did at this Last Supper was to give us his Body and Blood as a gift for all time. The bread and wine offered at this meal were now the Body and Blood of Christ. But the Eucharist can never be separated from what Jesus did on the cross. Each time the Eucharist is offered, the sacrifice of Jesus on the cross is really made present. In this way all the followers of Jesus Christ down through the ages are associated with his redeeming sacrifice.

Traditional site of the Last Supper, now a chapel

The Sacrifice of the Cross

All four gospels relate the details of Jesus' suffering and death: Matthew 26—27, Mark 14—15, Luke 22—23, and John 18—19. The story is all too familiar. After the Last Supper Jesus went to a garden to pray. Despite his fear and agony over what was to come, he did not run away. Having been betrayed by Judas for money, Jesus was arrested in the garden. Later he was brought before the high priest and accused of blasphemy because he claimed to be the Son of God. In the eyes of his fellow Jews, Jesus' claim of equality with God condemned him to death. Finally the Roman authorities allowed the death penalty to be carried out. Jesus was whipped, crowned with thorns, and mocked by Roman soldiers. Then he was led to his crucifixion like a common criminal.

We can hardly imagine what it was like for Jesus to undergo Roman crucifixion. Nailed to the cross, he must have been filled with incredible pain. Most victims of crucifixion actually suffocated to death because the muscles around their lungs were stretched so far that they could not breathe. It must have been that way for Jesus. Crucifixion was a horrible and humiliating way to die. But Jesus accepted this death for us. He died in agony and gave his life over to the Father because he was obedient to the will of his Father.

Jesus' death on the cross for us was a perfect sacrifice. It was not just the way he died, but why he died and what his death meant. His free offering of himself took away the sins of the world and brought about our redemption. His death was also the sacrifice of the new covenant that restored the human race to its friendship and communion with God. No one but a divine Person could have taken upon himself the sins of the whole world. Jesus' sacrifice was offered once and for all and surpassed all other sacrifices. Up to the time of the crucifixion, people offered sacrifices of grains and lambs and goats. From now on no other new sacrifices would ever be needed.

Why did Jesus offer himself in sacrifice for us? The answer is simple: out of love. That is why he came into the world and why he offered himself to the Father. The world had separated itself from God by sin. Jesus faced this evil head on and conquered it for all time. He became the sacrificial offering for sin for all people and for all time. That is why Jesus gave us the Eucharist as a memorial of his sacrifice on the cross. Through the Eucharist the sacrifice of the cross is made present for us today. Through the Eucharist we are associated with Jesus' redeeming sacrifice for us.

You may wish to read again the narrative of our Lord's passion and death in one of the four gospels.

CATHOLIC TEACHINGS

About the Priesthood

When referring to the institution of the Eucharist at the Last Supper, the *Catechism* states: "The Eucharist that Christ institutes at that moment will be the memorial of his sacrifice. Jesus includes the apostles in his own offering and bids them perpetuate it. By doing so, the Lord institutes his apostles as priests of the New Covenant" (611). This is the priesthood that has come down to us in the sacrament of Holy Orders through the apostolic succession and the laying on of hands. Through the ministry of priests, we are able to share in the Eucharist, the memorial of Christ's sacrifice on the cross.

At the time of Jesus, caves were used as tombs.

On the third day after his death, some of the women who followed Jesus went to the tomb to anoint his body. When they arrived there, they found the tomb empty! Where was he? He had risen from the dead! Soon the risen Jesus appeared to his closest disciples, including Mary Magdalene, other women, and the apostles. It was true! He had overcome death and was risen. But he had a glorified body; when Mary Magdalene first saw him, she did not recognize him (John 20:14–16). Unlike Lazarus and the widow's son, Jesus was not brought back to an ordinary earthly life. He was totally transformed. He had passed from death to a new life. No longer was Jesus subject to death. His glorified body was not limited by space and time.

The resurrection of Jesus from the dead is a historical fact verified by the empty tomb. Nevertheless, it is really a mystery of faith. That is one reason why the gospel accounts do not describe what took place at the resurrection. It was beyond a simple description. The gospels do, however, testify to the fact that the risen Christ appeared to his disciples. You may wish to read the resurrection accounts in Matthew 28, Mark 16, Luke 24, and John 20—21.

What more can we learn from the Church's reflection on the gospel accounts of the death and resurrection of Jesus? When Jesus died, he experienced a true death; his soul was separated from his body until he rose from the dead. But because he was a divine Person, his body did not

The Triduum Concludes

Jesus died on the cross. It was the custom for the Roman soldiers to break the legs of those crucified. But when they came to Jesus and saw that he was already dead, they did not break his legs; instead they pierced his side with a spear (John 19:33–34). Standing at the foot of the cross were Mary, the mother of Jesus, and several other women who had overcome their fear to be with him. The only apostle there was John, the beloved disciple. The rest of the apostles had run away and hid. They were afraid that they might suffer the same fate as their crucified Lord.

A friend of Jesus named Joseph of Arimathea asked the permission of Pilate to bury the body of Jesus. This Joseph was a member of the *Sanhedrin,* the ruling council of Judaism; it was made up of the high priest, elders, and scribes. Joseph took the body of Jesus and buried it in a tomb that had been carved out of rock. Everyone thought that the end had truly come, that Jesus was gone and would never be heard from again.

suffer the decay that is part of all human death. The risen Christ now transcended and surpassed human history.

Because his glorified body was no longer subject to the limitations of space and time, the risen Christ could appear to his apostles even through locked doors (John 20:19). Why did he appear only to his disciples, to people of faith? The risen Lord did not make a spectacle of himself; he did not appear to everyone. The resurrection was an event of faith, not a public show. It lies at the center of our faith. The resurrection is the confirmation of all that Jesus was and taught. This is what we celebrate during the Easter Vigil and on Easter Sunday. Jesus Christ is truly risen, as he said!

The Risen Christ

The risen Christ appeared to his disciples on many occasions, sharing with them what they would need to know for the future. One special appearance is recorded in John's Gospel. The risen Christ came before his apostles, who were hiding behind locked doors. Jesus said to them, "Peace be with you. As the Father has sent me, so I send you." Then Jesus breathed on them and said, "Receive the holy Spirit. Whose sins you forgive are forgiven them, and whose sins you retain are retained" (John 20:21–23). The risen Jesus had given his apostles the power to forgive sins.

Referring to this passage in John 20, the *Catechism* states, "By virtue of his divine authority he gives this power to men to exercise in his name" (1441). We already know that Jesus had the power to forgive sins. He was divine. Jesus entrusted the power of absolution to the apostolic ministry, but he requires of all his followers that they be instruments of forgiveness and reconciliation.

After a time, during which the risen Christ ate and drank with his disciples and taught them about the kingdom, he was ready to return to the Father. Before this took place, Jesus gathered the remaining eleven apostles and told them to continue his work. He said, "Go, therefore, and make disciples of all nations, baptizing them in the name of the Father, and of the Son, and of the holy Spirit, teaching them to observe all that I have commanded you. And behold, I am with you always, until the end of the age" (Matthew 28:19–20). Then Jesus was taken from their sight. Jesus ascended into heaven (Luke 24:51). The *ascension* was the entry of Jesus' humanity into divine glory. Jesus Christ preceded us into heaven. As members of his Church, we hope to join him one day.

 What does it mean for you to be a disciple of the risen Christ?

Scripture INSIGHT

The appearances of the risen Christ to his disciples include the following: to the disciples on the road to Emmaus (Luke 24:13–35), to the women who went to the tomb (Matthew 28:9–10), to Mary Magdalene (John 20:11–18), to the eleven apostles and other disciples (John 20:19–23, John 20:24–29, Matthew 28:16–20, and Acts 1:6–9). Read these passages. Explain how these disciples recognized the risen Jesus and what their reaction to him was.

PUTTING IT TOGETHER

things to think about

Were you surprised to learn that the details of Christ's resurrection are not contained in the gospels? Explain.

If you had been one of the apostles, do you think you would have had the strength to stay with Jesus during his passion and death? Explain.

things to share

After studying about Jesus' new and everlasting covenant, explain to someone why the cross is the most important symbol of Christianity.

How will your knowledge of the Last Supper and the crucifixion enhance your celebration of the Eucharist each Sunday?

WORDS TO REMEMBER

Find and define the following:

new commandment_____
_____
_____

ascension_____
_____
_____

OnLine
WITH THE PARISH

The Easter Triduum is the most important time in the Church year. Find out your parish schedule for the Triduum liturgies this year, and plan on attending and participating fully in these liturgies.

What do we mean by the paschal mystery?

1

What does the title *Son of Man* mean, and why is it so important in the New Testament?

2

What did Jesus mean when he spoke about the greatest commandment?

3

Why was Jesus' death on the cross a perfect sacrifice?

4

What do we mean when we say that the Eucharist is a memorial of Jesus' sacrifice on the cross?

5

Life in the Spirit

It was difficult for the apostle Thomas to believe that Jesus had risen from the dead. He was not with the others when Jesus first appeared to them. Later on Jesus showed himself to Thomas and challenged him to believe. When Thomas realized that it was really the risen Jesus, he exclaimed, "My Lord and my God!" (John 20:28). Many people use Thomas' words to profess their own faith in the risen Lord. Make his words your own, especially after you receive Christ in the Eucharist.

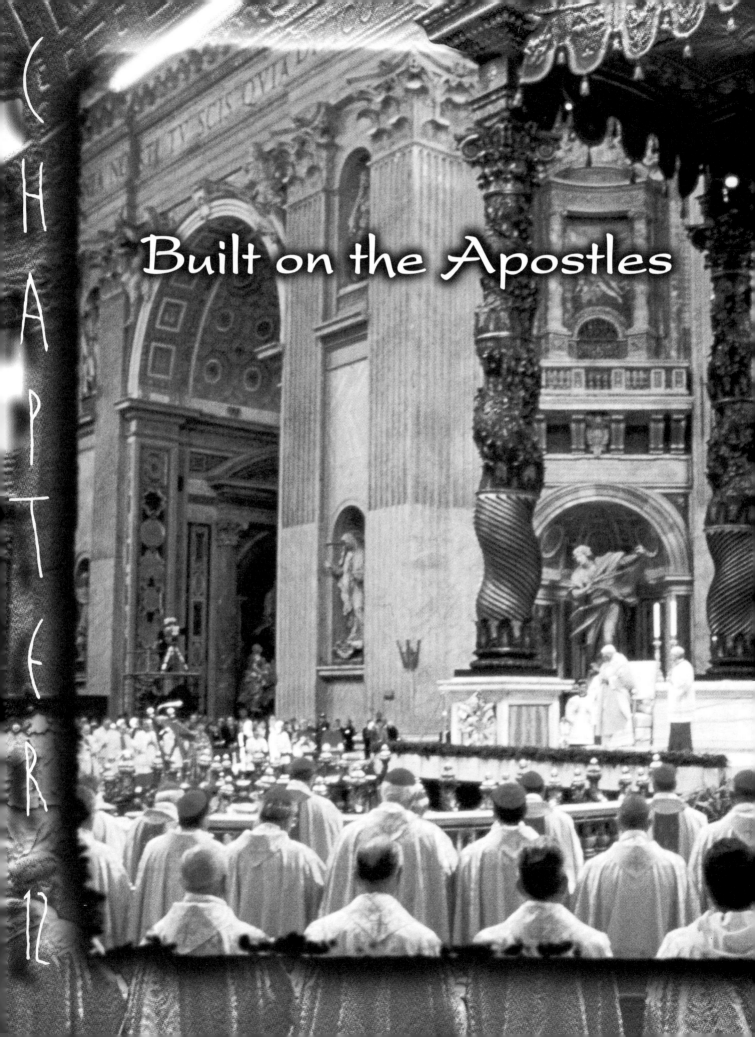

CHAPTER 12

Built on the Apostles

You founded your Church
on the apostles to stand firm for ever.

Preface of the Apostles II

When did the Church begin? How did it start?
A second-century Christian writer made a startling
statement. He said that the Church was the first in
all God's creation, that "the whole world was
created just for the sake of the Church."
What do you think the writer meant?

The coming of the Holy Spirit

The Origin of the Church

What this author was saying was that the Church
was part of God's plan from all eternity. Through the
Church God planned to share the divine life to which
he called all people through his Son. We now turn to
Scripture to help us understand the Church.

Old Testament Preparation Preparation for the Church began long before the time of Jesus and the New Testament. The Church, the people of God, was formed gradually over many centuries. God's plan of salvation began to unfold when he called Abraham to be the father of many nations. Later God made a covenant with his people Israel, a nation made up of twelve tribes. They would be the sign of the future time when God would gather people of every nation to himself, when God would make a new and everlasting covenant.

A new covenant was clearly on the mind of the prophet Jeremiah when he announced, "The days are coming, says the LORD, when I will make a new covenant with the house of Israel" (31:31). This is the new and everlasting covenant that was brought about by Jesus.

Call of the Apostles When Jesus began his public ministry, he called people to follow him, and those who responded became his disciples. One day, according to Luke 6:12–16, Jesus went up to a mountain and spent a whole night in prayer. The next day he called his disciples to himself and chose twelve to be his apostles. They would be the new Israel. Just as the twelve tribes had been the foundation of the old covenant, so these twelve apostles would be the foundation of the new covenant. Here are the names of the Twelve:

- Simon, later called Peter
- Andrew, Simon Peter's brother
- James, son of Zebedee
- John, James's brother
- Philip, a fisherman
- Bartholomew, also known as Nathanael
- Thomas, whose name means "twin"
- Matthew, a tax collector
- James, son of Alphaeus
- Thaddaeus, also known as Jude
- Simon the Zealot
- Judas Iscariot, Jesus' betrayer.

The list of the apostles' names can be found in Matthew 10:2–4, Mark 3:16–19, Luke 6:14–16, and Acts 1:13. The word *apostle* is a Greek word meaning "one who is sent." The importance of being an apostle comes from being sent by Christ. As someone who was sent, an apostle was the ambassador of Christ with full authority to act in his name. When he was commissioning the Twelve, Jesus said, "As the Father has sent me, so I send you" (John 20:21). Jesus also said, "Whoever receives you receives me, and whoever receives me receives the one who sent me" (Matthew 10:40).

Revealed by the Holy Spirit With the resurrection of Jesus, a new age began in the world. All the foundations of the Church that Christ had laid now came to fulfillment. The Holy Spirit embraced the disciples of Jesus and brought into being the Church that Jesus had promised.

How did this happen? The risen Christ had promised to send his apostles a Helper, an Advocate. This was the Holy Spirit, the third Person of the Blessed Trinity. The coming of the Holy Spirit to Jesus' disciples is described in a dramatic way in the Acts of the Apostles. On the day of Pentecost, when the disciples were gathered in a place by themselves, the Spirit came upon them in what seemed like tongues of fire (Acts 2:3).

Suddenly the disciples of Jesus were filled with courage. No longer were they afraid. They went out to preach the good news of Jesus Christ. The descent of the Holy Spirit upon them had ushered in the age of the Church. From that time, down through the centuries, the disciples of Jesus would meet their Lord in and through the Church. The Father had sent the Son to earth to accomplish the work of salvation and sanctification. The Holy Spirit would continue that work through the Church until the end of time. On that first Pentecost the Church of Christ was revealed to the world, and its work began.

 What surprises you most about the statement that the world was created for the Church?

The Primacy of Peter

Immediately after the coming of the Holy Spirit upon the Church, the apostles went out from the place where they were hiding and began to proclaim that Jesus was the Messiah. Peter, representing the other apostles, was the first to stand up and speak to the people. Many had gathered in Jerusalem from every corner of the earth. Why was Peter the first to speak for the new community of the Church?

The gospels indicate that Peter held a unique position among all the disciples of Jesus. He was the first to accept the call to discipleship. After Jesus had been baptized by John the Baptist and had gone out to the desert to prepare for his ministry, he called his first disciples. As Jesus was walking along the shore of the Sea of Galilee, he saw two fishermen. One of them was Simon, later called Peter, and with him was his brother Andrew. Jesus said to them, "Come after me, and I will make you fishers of men" (Matthew 4:19). And they immediately followed him.

Even though he was a married man (Matthew 8:14) and had a trade of his own, Simon Peter left his fishing nets to join Jesus. From the very beginning Jesus saw in Peter special qualities of leadership and later chose him to be the leader of the Twelve. Peter is the most frequently mentioned apostle in the gospels. In fact, wherever lists of the twelve apostles appear in the New Testament, Peter is always listed first.

Why was Peter singled out in this way? Jesus must have recognized in him something uncommon, a strength and generosity of heart that were characteristic of this tough fisherman. One day when Jesus asked his disciples who they thought he was, Simon was quick to take the lead and give a reply. He said, "You are the Messiah, the Son of the living God." When Jesus heard this, he said, "Blessed are you, Simon son of Jonah. For flesh and blood has not revealed this to you, but my heavenly Father. And so I say to you, you are Peter, and upon this rock I will build my church" (Matthew 16:16–18).

The Calling of the Apostles Peter and Andrew, Duccio di Buoninsegna, 14th century

Jesus was giving Simon a new name, *Peter,* which means "rock." Peter had recognized Jesus' identity as the Christ, a title that later was added to Jesus' name. Now in the same way, Jesus was recognizing Peter as the rock foundation of his Church and was giving him a title to add to his name. That explains why he was frequently called Simon Peter.

Then Jesus said to Peter, "I will give you the keys to the kingdom of heaven. Whatever you bind on earth shall be bound in heaven; and whatever you loose on earth shall be loosed in heaven" (Matthew 16:19). Later, after his resurrection, Jesus said to Peter, "Feed my lambs" and "Feed my sheep" (John 21:15–18). When Jesus spoke to Peter in these ways, he spoke to Peter alone. Only Peter received the keys of the Church, a symbol of authority. The other apostles together with Peter were to have the power to govern the Church (Matthew 18:18), but Peter alone was its rock and chief shepherd.

appearance changed. He was transfigured before them: "His face shone like the sun and his clothes became white as light." At that instant the apostles also saw Moses and Elijah talking with Jesus. The only one to speak was Peter. He said, "Lord, it is good that we are here" (Matthew 17:2, 4). Even though Peter did not yet understand what this transfiguration meant, he nevertheless had the courage to speak.

The picture that Scripture gives is clear: Peter was the first disciple chosen by Jesus. He was given full authority by Jesus to be the leader of the early Church. He was the foundation upon which Christ would build the Church. In succeeding generations the role of Peter and the "shoes of the fisherman" would be filled by the pope.

Think of ways that the Holy Father, the successor of Peter today, exercises leadership in the Church.

The Witness of Peter

The gospels are filled with many accounts describing Peter's position in the circle of disciples. Time and again it is Peter who stands out in the group. For example, in Matthew 14:28, only Peter is courageous enough to try to imitate Jesus by walking on the water. In the story of the miraculous catch of fish (Luke 5:4–11), Jesus and Peter discuss putting out for deep water and lowering the nets for a catch. Peter takes the chief role in this story, too.

Peter was also privileged to be among what we might call the inner circle of Jesus' disciples. Often he would accompany Jesus with James and John to special places. One of the most important times was at the *transfiguration,* when Jesus gave a glimpse of his divinity to these three apostles. In a brief moment Jesus'

Scripture Insight

Peter was by no means perfect. He needed to learn what it meant to be a faithful follower of Jesus. That is why Jesus spoke sternly to Peter on more than one occasion. Once Jesus said, "Get behind me, Satan. You are thinking not as God does, but as human beings do" (Mark 8:33). Remember, too, that Peter fell asleep in the garden during Jesus' agony. He even denied Jesus after his arrest. But Peter learned from his mistakes and knew what it meant to be one who serves others, as Jesus taught. That is why Jesus called him the rock.

A People with Leaders

Judas Iscariot, one of the original twelve apostles chosen by Jesus, had betrayed him for thirty pieces of silver. Full of regret for what he had done, Judas returned the money and went out and hanged himself (Matthew 27:5). After Jesus' ascension the early Church felt that it was important to replace Judas. Jesus himself had chosen twelve apostles, symbolic of the twelve tribes of Israel. The Church was to be the new Israel; it would be the result of the new covenant in Jesus' Blood. So the apostles gathered to choose a replacement for Judas and bring their number back to twelve.

What qualifications would this replacement need? Peter said, "It is necessary that one of the men who accompanied us the whole time the Lord Jesus came and went among us, beginning from the baptism of John until the day on which he was taken up from us, become with us a witness to his resurrection" (Acts 1:21–22). After praying, they chose a man named Matthias. He had been one of Jesus' first disciples and had witnessed all the important events in Jesus' life. So he had all the qualifications to be an apostolic leader of the Church of Christ.

What is the Church? The root meaning of the word *Church* is "belonging to the Lord." In Scripture it means "a people called together." The Church is the assembly of those chosen by God in Jesus Christ, the assembly of God's people. Being the Church involves not only being the gathered community but also the process of gathering together. The Church, therefore, is not only an established group but also an event: people coming together especially for the purpose of worshiping God and serving others.

An Apostolic Ministry

After Pentecost the eleven original apostles and Matthias began to proclaim the good news of Jesus everywhere. With great courage they carried out the Lord's command to "make disciples of all nations" (Matthew 28:19); they followed the promptings of the Holy Spirit and established local Churches wherever they went. They did not stay in any one place, however, because they were leaders of the whole Church.

The twelve apostles shared their work with others in the wider ministry of founding and organizing these local Churches. Sometimes these other apostolic leaders, like Paul, were also called "apostles" even though they were not a part of the original Twelve (2 Corinthians 8:23). But other names, such as "prophet" and "evangelist," were also used to describe them (Ephesians 4:11). The reason is that official titles had not yet been determined by the Church.

Once a local Church became established, the apostolic leaders moved on. But they chose and left behind local Church officers, whom they had ordained by the laying on of hands (2 Timothy 1:6). These men, too, were called by a number of different titles: "pastor" or "teacher" or "presbyter" (priest, elder) or "bishop" (overseer). The words seemed to have been used interchangeably (Titus 1:5–7). Assisted by deacons, these local officers presided over their Churches under the authority of the apostles, prophets, and evangelists. But their official titles, like those of the apostolic leaders, had not yet been determined.

After the Church began to spread around the world, the general traveling ministry of the apostolic leaders became less necessary. It gradually died out as the apostolic leaders passed away. Some of them may have settled in local Churches, as we know James had done in Jerusalem and Timothy in Ephesus (Acts 21:18; 1 Timothy 1:3).

In any event the title of bishop became reserved only for the successors of the apostolic leaders and the title of presbyter (priest) for the other local officers. The title of deacon remained unchanged.

The ministry of the apostles, therefore, was continued and assured in the ministry of the local bishops. They were the successors of the apostles. These men were the vital link to the apostles and thus to Christ himself. By A.D. 110 Ignatius of Antioch could speak of the threefold ministry of bishop, presbyter (priest), and deacon as "established in the farthest parts of the earth." It is remarkable that all of this happened in such a short time. Through the laying on of hands, we have the same threefold ministry today.

The story of the selection of the first deacons of the Church is told in Acts 6:1–7. Take a few minutes to read this passage and to think about the ministry of deacons in your parish.

CATHOLIC ID The Church reminds us that every baptized member of the Church is called to the work of evangelization, not just ordained ministers. *Evangelization* means bringing the good news to every person and to all parts of the human experience. Each one of us shares in that responsibility wherever we are.

Open-air theater, Ephesus, site of a riot against Paul's preaching (Acts 19:23–40)

The Early Church

The early Church community was well aware of its close relationship with the original Twelve. These were the men who had been the constant companions of Jesus. He was their personal friend. Who more than they realized how likable Jesus was, what a warm and caring individual he was? These apostles were also firsthand witnesses to the miracles of Jesus and to his resurrection. It was they whom Jesus sent out in his name, just as Jesus himself had been sent by his Father (John 13:20).

As God's chosen representatives the apostles were to be listened to (2 Corinthians 5:20). They did not receive their commission from the Church; they received it from the Lord. The apostles were "God's co-workers" (1 Corinthians 3:9). They baptized, celebrated the Eucharist in the breaking of the bread, and laid their hands on others in conferring the Holy Spirit and calling others to ministry. They forgave sins in God's name; and with the fullness of Christ's power, they even worked miracles (Acts 2:43).

They had the right to be received as Christ himself (Galatians 4:14). As such they could demand the obedience of the Church community, which they led in the name of Jesus Christ (1 Corinthians 14:37).

The apostles presided over the community not as rulers over subjects, however, but as fellow members of the Church. Theirs was a ministry of service; they were to be the servants of the Church. As commanded by Jesus himself, they were to be models of service. Jesus had said, "Whoever wishes to be great among you will be your servant; whoever wishes to be first among you will be the slave of all. For the Son of Man did not come to be served but to serve and to give his life as a ransom for many" (Mark 10:43–45).

Apostle to the Gentiles

When we read the Acts of the Apostles and the letters of the New Testament, we cannot help noticing the special importance of one man: Paul. Originally called Saul, Paul was an educated man and a Roman citizen. Fervent in his Jewish faith, he

146

at first hated the followers of Jesus Christ and set out to destroy them. One day on his way to persecute Christians in Damascus, Paul had a vision of Christ, who said to him, "Saul, Saul, why are you persecuting me?" (Acts 9:4). With this experience Paul began to realize that in persecuting Christians, he was persecuting Christ himself. Perhaps it was at this very moment that Paul began to think of the Church of Christ as the body of Christ.

 Read the account of Paul's conversion and Baptism in Acts 9:1–19.

Soon Paul became one of the most active of the apostolic leaders. He traveled all over the Gentile world, spreading the good news. For this reason he became known as the Apostle to the Gentiles. His activity, however, was not appreciated by everyone at first. Some people thought that Gentile converts should first become Jews and follow Jewish laws before becoming Christians.

The Conversion of Saint Paul, engraving after Gustave Doré, late 19th century

CATHOLIC TEACHINGS

About the Church

Today where do we find the Church of Christ that is referred to in the New Testament? The bishops at the Second Vatican Council (1962–1965) gave a clear answer. They said that the Church of Christ can be found in its essential fullness in the Catholic Church: "This is the unique Church of Christ which in the Creed we avow as one, holy, catholic, and apostolic. . . . This Church, constituted and organized in the world as a society, subsists in the Catholic Church, which is governed by the successor of Peter and by the bishops in union with that successor, although many elements of sanctification and of truth can be found outside her visible structure" (*Church*, 8). Thus the council teaching is that the Church of Christ "subsists" in the Catholic Church. This means that the Church of Christ is truly present in its essential completeness in the Catholic Church.

In Acts 15:1–35 we read that a council was called in Jerusalem to decide this important issue. Paul was one of the principal players in this first Church council, which probably was held about A.D. 50. There, in support of Paul, Peter formulated the fundamental principle that Gentiles were not bound by Jewish law. Contrary to what some thought, the Gentiles were to have equal access to Christ along with the Jews. After the description of the Council of Jerusalem until the end of the Acts of the Apostles, the story of the Church's beginning centers on the missionary journeys of Paul to the Gentiles. Like the other apostles, Paul spent the rest of his life planting the seeds of the Church of Christ throughout the world.

PUTTING IT TOGETHER

things to think about

Why do you think Jesus chose Peter to be the leader of the apostles? What qualities should such a leader have?

Why do you think Paul referred to the apostles as God's co-workers?

things to share

Isn't it amazing that the structure of the Church we have today is rooted in the earliest Church community? Share with a friend why this is so.

Explain to someone why Paul is properly called the Apostle to the Gentiles.

WORDS TO REMEMBER

Find and define the following:

apostle _____
_____
_____

Church _____
_____
_____

OnLine
WITH THE PARISH

Many parishes are named after one of the twelve apostles. Choose one of the apostles, and do some research on his life. Share what you learn with your group.

Name as many of the twelve apostles as you can.

1

What do we mean when we say that the Church was revealed by the Holy Spirit on Pentecost?

2

Describe the position that Peter held among Jesus' first disciples.

3

Why was the Council of Jerusalem so important?

4

Life
in the Spirit

One of the liturgical prayers of the Church calls the apostles the "living gospel" that all people can hear. Have you ever thought of yourself and your life as a type of living gospel for others to "hear" each day? Take a few moments to ask the Holy Spirit to help you grow as a "living gospel" for others in your family, school, and neighborhood.

Why does the Church teach that bishops are the successors of the apostles?

4

CHAPTER 13

A People Set Apart

You are the salt of the earth.
But if salt loses its taste, with
what can it be seasoned?

Matthew 5:13

In His Image, William Zdinak, 20th century

*If you were asked to describe the Church
in several words, what would you say?*

New Testament Images

The writers of the New Testament used picturesque language to describe the Church. We call their colorful descriptions *images of the Church.* These images are important not only because they help us to understand the Church of New Testament times but also because they describe how the Church sees itself today.

Some of the images found in the New Testament are like windows that give us a small glimpse into the nature of the Church. Other images are like doors that open wide and let us see the deeper meaning of the Church of Christ. Not all the images are of equal importance, but they are nonetheless too important for us to ignore.

In one way or another, all the images point to the intimate relationship between Christ and the members of the Church. Look at the way this close and intimate relationship is brought out in the following images. The Church is described as:

- vine and branches (John 15:1–5)
- bride of Christ (2 Corinthians 11:2)
- salt of the earth (Matthew 5:13)
- one loaf (1 Corinthians 10:17)
- God's building (1 Corinthians 3:9)
- household of God (Ephesians 2:19)
- light of the world (Matthew 5:14)
- temple of the Holy Spirit (1 Corinthians 3:16)
- sheepfold (John 10:1–5).

These are only a few of the images of the Church in the New Testament. Some people have counted as many as a hundred. As important as all the images of the Church are, two stand out. These are the images of the Church as the people of God and the Church as the body of Christ.

People of God Many Christians forget that we have been *chosen by God* to be his adopted children, brothers and sisters of Jesus Christ (Ephesians 1:3–6). We are God's "chosen ones" (Colossians 3:12). God chose us first, before we ever chose him. This is the great privilege we receive at Baptism, when we are born anew as adopted sons and daughters of God. God's choice and our Baptism bring us into a community, the people of God. We are therefore a people set apart. The author of the First Letter of Peter says that we are now "God's people" (2:10). He also says that we are "a chosen race, a royal priesthood, a holy nation, a people of his own" (2:9).

Because we are a people set apart by God, we have been chosen to live a certain way. We are to be temples of the Holy Spirit; we are to live as sons and daughters of our heavenly Father. We belong to a people chosen in Christ. This means that we are to live according to Christ's command to love one another as he loved us. As a people set apart, we also have a mission in the world. We are to be the salt of the earth and the light of the world, bringing the message of Christ everywhere. This is the Church, the people of God, "the seed and beginning" of God's kingdom (*Catechism*, 541).

Body of Christ The Church is the people of God, but *the people of God as the body of Christ*. What a wonderful image! We are the people of God in Jesus Christ, not without him. We are his body, and he is our head, the head of the Church. It was Paul who gave us this rich image of the Church. In his First Letter to the Corinthians, he says, "As a body is one though it has many parts, and all the parts of the body, though many, are one body, so also Christ" (12:12).

Just as each part of the human body has a specific function, so each member of Christ's body has a special role in the Church. There is only one head but many members. All the members are one in Christ, joined together by the power of the Holy Spirit. Paul also said, "For in one Spirit we were all baptized into one body, whether Jews or Greeks, slaves or free persons, and we were all given to drink of one Spirit" (1 Corinthians 12:13).

As members of Christ's body, we receive our life from Christ himself. We live through him, with him, and in him. Through the power of the Holy Spirit, especially in the sacraments, the risen Christ nourishes his body, the Church. There can be no more intimate connection between us and Christ than in the sacrament of sacraments, the Eucharist: "Whoever eats my flesh and drinks my blood remains in me and I in him" (John 6:56).

Look again at the images of the Church given in this lesson. Choose one that is especially appealing to you, and tell why.

A Worshiping People

We do not have to spend much time with the New Testament before we realize that the early Church was a community at prayer. The Acts of the Apostles reminds us that the early Christians got together in their homes each day for the breaking of the bread (2:46). They did what Jesus had told them to do at the Last Supper in memory of him when he broke the bread and gave it to his disciples. This "breaking of the bread" was another name for the Eucharist.

Saint Paul explained that this Eucharist was the Body and Blood of the Lord. Those who came to receive the Eucharist had to do so worthily because they were receiving Christ himself (1 Corinthians 11:27–29). From the very beginning of the Church, the community recognized the real presence of the risen Christ in the Eucharist. Paul challenged the early Christians on this matter. He said to them, "The cup of blessing that we bless, is it not a participation in the blood of Christ? The bread that we break, is it not a participation in the body of Christ?" (1 Corinthians 10:16).

The Eucharist became the central action that defined the Christian community. But the early Church also used other sacred rituals, or sacred actions, in its worship. These, too, are mentioned frequently in the New Testament. The first and most recognizable was the ritual of baptizing. When people heard the preaching of the apostles and wanted to become disciples of Christ and members of the Church, they were baptized.

This ritual washing was a rebirth to new life by water and the Holy Spirit. Paul described it this way in his Letter to the Romans: "Are you unaware that we who were baptized into Christ Jesus were baptized into his death? We were indeed buried with him through baptism into death, so that, just as Christ was raised from the dead by the glory of the Father, we too might live in newness of life" (6:3–4). This newness of life is the life of grace.

Baptism, then, is the entrance into the Christian life and the beginning of one's relationship with Christ. Through Baptism people become adopted children of God in Christ and members of the Church (Galatians 3:26–27).

Other Rituals

Another important ritual we read about in the New Testament is the ancient gesture of the laying on of hands. By this action the apostles conferred the gift of the Holy Spirit on those who were baptized (Acts 8:14–17). This action also signified the conferring of authority on those who were the co-workers and successors of the apostles. Hands were laid on Paul (Acts 9:17). The apostles laid their hands on those chosen to be the first deacons of the Church (Acts 6:6). The First and Second Letters to Timothy speak of this laying on of hands for the ordained ministry of the Church (1 Timothy 4:14; 2 Timothy 1:6).

There were other ritual gestures of healing for the sick. In the Letter to James, a gesture of anointing is mentioned. There we read, "Is anyone among you sick? He should summon the presbyters of the church, and they should pray over him and anoint [him] with oil in the name of the Lord, and the prayer of faith will save the sick person, and the Lord will raise him up. If he has committed any sins, he will be forgiven" (James 5:14–15). The Letter of James then speaks about the confessing of sins in the early Church (5:16). As we have already seen, Peter and the apostles were given the power to forgive sins by Christ himself (Matthew 16:18, 18:18; John 20:21–23).

Marriage was another sacred action recognized in the New Testament. In the Letter to the Ephesians, Paul wrote about marriage. He compared the close relationship between a man and a woman in marriage to Christ and his body, the Church (Ephesians 5:21–33). Jesus himself attended a wedding feast in Cana of Galilee.

It is clear, then, that in the New Testament we find the foundation for what would eventually be called the seven sacraments. These seven are Baptism, Confirmation, Eucharist, Reconciliation, Anointing of the Sick, Holy Orders, and Matrimony. By the power of the Holy Spirit, the risen Christ is present to his Church through these sacred rituals and actions. This is the way Christ nourishes his body, the Church. This is the way in which the Church shares most deeply in the mystery of salvation and offers praise to God the Father.

In which sacraments have you already participated? In which have you witnessed others participating?

Scripture UPDATE

The New Testament epistles can be difficult for some people to read because they are not like modern letters. Modern letters either are chatty and filled with light conversation or deal with business matters. The epistles, on the other hand, devoted a lot of space to explaining Christian doctrine and to urging a community to be strong in living the Christian life. Most New Testament letters were written to Christian communities or their leaders. They were meant to be read aloud as the community gathered. All of them give us a glimpse into concerns important to the early Church—and to the Church in every age.

Living in Christ

The concerns of the New Testament writers were not limited to prayer and worship or the passing on of belief in Christ and his Church. They were also interested in the ways that Christians put their faith into practice in their daily lives. Faith without good works was declared to be useless:

> If a brother or sister has nothing to wear and has no food for the day, and one of you says to them, "Go in peace, keep warm, and eat well," but you do not give them the necessities of the body, what good is it? So also faith of itself, if it does not have works, is dead.
> James 2:15–17

In this passage James is saying that faith is so important that we cannot hide it. Faith is not like a museum piece that is only admired. Rather it must be used and put into practice. This obligation extends to our attitudes about others as well. This is what gospel living is all about: It is about justice, forgiveness, love, mercy, and all the things that Jesus taught us. A good example of this can be seen in a conversation Jesus had with Peter one day. Peter had asked Jesus how many times we have to forgive others when they hurt us. Would seven times be enough? Jesus answered, "I say to you, not seven times but seventy-seven times" (Matthew 18:22).

Jesus was telling Peter something very important. For a follower of Christ, forgiveness can have no limit whatsoever. That is why he used the number seventy-seven. Seven, the biblical number that symbolizes perfection and completion, must be multiplied over and over. Forgiveness is something to be practiced, not just thought about.

How can a Christian person do this? How can we be so forgiving, so just, so merciful? What makes it possible? Only the grace of God and the realization that we are so loved by God. This is why Jesus came into the world. In John we read, "For God so loved the world that he gave his only Son, so that everyone who believes in him might not perish but might have eternal life" (3:16). Once we realize that God loves us so much, we can share that same love with others. That is why Jesus could say that we should love our enemies.

Sometimes it seems easier to love outsiders than to love those in our own community. Jesus, however, insisted on the harmony that should exist in the community. He taught that anger and jealousy can be destructive and must be dealt with. Jesus said, "If you bring your gift to the altar, and there recall that your brother has anything against you, leave your gift there at the altar, go first and be reconciled with your brother, and then come and offer your gift" (Matthew 5:23–24).

A Prescription for Love

Jesus extended his teaching to the question of judging others and criticizing them for faults that we ourselves have. Jesus said, "Why do you notice the splinter in your brother's eye, but do not perceive the wooden beam in your own eye? How can you say to your brother, 'Let me remove that splinter from your eye,' while the wooden beam is in your eye? You hypocrite, remove the wooden beam from your eye first; then you will see clearly to remove the splinter from your brother's eye" (Matthew 7:3–5).

One of the things that Jesus seems to have had no patience with was hypocrisy in others, especially in his followers. *Hypocrisy* means putting on a false appearance of virtue or goodness. When Jesus spoke of the splinter and the beam, he was saying that we should not judge others until we first take a good look at ourselves to see where we need improvement.

Everything that Jesus taught us about putting our faith into practice can be summarized under the heading of love. All the writers of the New Testament were concerned about the ways in which we fulfill Jesus' command to love. Paul had his prescription, too. The words that he wrote to the Christians in Corinth have become one of the favorite passages of Scripture over the centuries:

"Love is patient, love is kind. It is not jealous, [love] is not pompous, it is not inflated, it is not rude, it does not seek its own interests, it is not quick-tempered, it does not brood over injury, it does not rejoice over wrongdoing but rejoices with the truth. It bears all things, believes all things, hopes all things, endures all things. Love never fails" (1 Corinthians 13:4–8).

Ask yourself in what ways you might continue to grow as a loving follower of Christ. Write your thoughts in your journal.

CATHOLIC ID

Each year on the feast of All Saints, Catholics hear some beautiful passages of the New Testament proclaimed. One of the most vivid, depicting the saints in heaven singing the praises of God, comes from Revelation 7:9–10. It reminds us of our belief in the communion of saints, the union of all the Church members. The *communion of saints* is the unity and cooperation of the members of the Church on earth with those in heaven and those in purgatory.

The Christian Vocation

Through the sacrament of Baptism, we share in the divine life of the risen Lord. Through Baptism all the members of the Church have the same vocation: to live as disciples of Jesus Christ. The challenge to live out this Christian vocation has not changed since New Testament times. It was the same for Peter and Paul, for the Corinthians and the Ephesians. It will continue to be the same for Christians of the twenty-first century and every century thereafter.

How can the Christian vocation be the same for every century? Circumstances may change, but the teaching of Jesus remains the same. The Beatitudes, for example, were the same for the first Christians as they are for us today. And it is in the Beatitudes that we find the heart of Jesus' message.

The word *beatitude* means "happiness." In the Beatitudes Jesus gave us a short list of prescriptions for living a happy life in harmony with God. The list names those qualities or virtues that each follower of Christ must strive for in life. Will living the Beatitudes help us to be happy? For the Christian the Beatitudes are the only way to achieve true and lasting happiness. They show us the way to God's own happiness—the happiness, or beatitude, of the Blessed Trinity itself. Therefore, the Beatitudes not only contribute to our happiness on earth but also lead us to the fullness of happiness, or beatitude, in heaven. This is the final end to which God calls us.

 Study the list of the Beatitudes as found on page 159.

Jesus, Our Example

Jesus not only taught us the Beatitudes; he lived them. In fact he is our best example of what it means to have a "beatitude attitude." Instead of searching for power and authority and riches, Jesus sought out those who lived at the edges of society: the rejected, the segregated, and those who suffered injustices of all sorts. He did not come to condemn sinners; he came to bring them mercy.

All types of people pressed in upon Jesus, seeking to be comforted by him. Jesus had compassion for all of them: "At the sight of the crowds, his heart was moved with pity for them because they were troubled and abandoned, like sheep without a shepherd" (Matthew 9:36). Acceptance and understanding were the constant attitudes of Jesus toward those who approached him. These included criminals, lepers, the sick and suffering, sinners, prostitutes, those possessed with demons, and even those who condemned him to death.

For members of the Church, the example of Jesus has practical consequences. That is why we engage in missionary activity. It is why we are involved in the care of the sick in hospitals and nursing homes. It is why we care for runaways and for unwed mothers. It is why we challenge politicians and those in government to see to the needs of the most defenseless members of society. It is why parishes reach out to the poor and homeless through organizations such as the Saint Vincent de Paul Society. No one should be left out. We are to care for unborn children and the frail elderly. This is truly what it means to practice our faith and to live out the Christian vocation.

Jesus invited everyone to this vocation. He knew it would be a challenge, and that is why he told us we would have to take up our cross in order to follow him. But he also promised to be with us and to lift us up in times of fear, anxiety, and need. He said, "Come to me, all you who labor and are burdened, and I will give you rest. Take my yoke upon you and learn from me, for I am meek and humble of heart; and you will find rest for yourselves. For my yoke is easy, and my burden light" (Matthew 11:28–30).

The Beatitudes

Blessed are the poor in spirit,
    for theirs is the kingdom of heaven.
Blessed are they who mourn,
    for they will be comforted.
Blessed are the meek,
    for they will inherit the land.
Blessed are they who hunger and thirst
        for righteousness,
    for they will be satisfied.
Blessed are the merciful,
    for they will be shown mercy.
Blessed are the clean of heart,
    for they will see God.
Blessed are the peacemakers,
    for they will be called children of God.
Blessed are they who are persecuted
        for the sake of righteousness,
    for theirs is the kingdom of heaven.
Matthew 5:3–10

CATHOLIC TEACHINGS

About the Beatitudes

The Church teaches that "true happiness is not found in riches or well-being, in human fame or power, or in any human achievement—however beneficial it may be—such as science, technology, and art, or indeed in any creature, but in God alone, the source of every good and of all love" (Catechism, 1723).

things to think about

Why do you think it is so important to understand that the Church is *the people of God as the body of Christ*?

Can we still describe the Church today as a community at prayer, as the early Church was? Why or why not?

things to share

How many of the approximately one hundred New Testament images of the Church can you name? Which ones would you like to explain to others?

How would you respond to someone who says that what you believe is what counts, not what you do? Which part of the New Testament would you use in your response?

WORDS TO REMEMBER

Find and define the following:

images of the Church _____
_____
_____

Beatitudes _____
_____
_____

OnLine

WITH THE PARISH

Our parish is our home in the Church. It is the place and the community in which we live out our Christian vocation. How is your parish challenging you today to live up to your vocation? How will you respond to the challenge?

Why can we describe the followers of Christ as a people set apart?

1

Why is it true to say that in the New Testament we find the foundation of the seven sacraments? Give one example.

2

How can the Christian vocation be the same for every century?

3

Choose one beatitude, and put it into your own words.

4

Name one way that the New Testament epistles differ from modern letters.

5

Life in the Spirit

The 1997 World Youth Day was celebrated in Paris, France. While participating in this event, Pope John Paul II beatified Frédéric Ozanam, the founder of the Saint Vincent de Paul Society. Beatification is the step before canonization as a saint. Find out all you can about Blessed Frédéric Ozanam and the society he founded. Pray that you, too, can be known for your faith and for your good works.

CHAPTER 14

Come, Lord Jesus

The grace of the Lord Jesus be with all.

Revelation 22:21

Christians often speak about the second coming of Christ to the world. What does this "second coming" mean to you?

First and Second Comings

People of faith need to understand the difference between the first and second comings. The first coming of Jesus was at his birth, when he came to Mary and to the world. We call this the incarnation, when the second Person of the Blessed Trinity took on our human nature. But in the New Testament, we also learn about the second coming. The *second coming* is the future return of Christ in glory to judge the living and the dead and to bring to an end the world as we know it. This second coming is also referred to as the parousia. The word *parousia* means "coming."

Born of a Woman We cannot talk about the first coming of Jesus without talking about his mother, Mary. She is the woman chosen and made holy by the Blessed Trinity to be the Mother of God and the Mother of the Church. In a beautiful passage from the New Testament, Paul wrote about Mary, who was chosen by the Trinity:

> When the fullness of time had come, God sent his Son, born of a woman, born under the law, to ransom those under the law, so that we might receive adoption. As proof that you are children, God sent the spirit of his Son into our hearts, crying out, "Abba, Father!"
> Galatians 4:4–6

The woman Paul was speaking about in this passage was Mary, who had been embraced by all the Persons of the Trinity. This was Mary, who was greeted by an angel as full of grace, as God's favored one (Luke 1:28). This was Mary, the handmaid of the Lord, who said yes to God's invitation to be the mother of his only Son (Luke 1:38). Conceived by the Holy Spirit, Jesus received his humanity totally from the Blessed Virgin Mary. Together with Joseph she is the one who gave him his human upbringing. She surrounded him with tender loving care and taught him by her example. With her whole heart, Mary trusted in God and gave herself completely to the life and work of her son. That is why we say that she is the first disciple of the Lord.

What relationship did Jesus want us to have with his mother? The answer becomes clear when we read John's Gospel. As Jesus was dying on the cross, he looked down and saw his mother and the disciple whom he loved standing at the foot of the cross. He said to Mary, "Behold, your son." Then to the disciple he said, "Behold, your mother" (John 19:26, 27). Literally Jesus was asking the beloved disciple to take care of his mother. By extension the Church has understood this passage to mean that Mary was given to the whole Church to be our mother, too. That is why we honor her as the Mother of the Church.

The Parousia Since the earliest days of the Church, Christians have been waiting in hope for the second coming of Christ (1 Thessalonians 1:10).

This waiting and hoping is a theme that runs through the New Testament. However, no one knew exactly when this second coming would occur. Jesus himself warned his disciples that it was not for them to know the day or the hour.

One day Jesus was talking with his disciples about the end of history, the end of time. All of them, no doubt, were curious to know when this would occur. Jesus anticipated their question. He warned them and all his followers not to be fooled by false prophets and those who pretend to have all the answers. About the end of the world and his second coming, he said, "But of that day or hour, no one knows, neither the angels in heaven, nor the Son, but only the Father. Be watchful! Be alert! You do not know when the time will come" (Mark 13:32–33).

For Catholics the message of Jesus is clear. No one knows when the end will come. That is why Catholics do not stand on street corners with posters announcing that the end of the world is near. We do not want to be among the false prophets about whom Jesus warned. We are simply to grow as his followers and prepare for his second coming. Each Sunday we profess in the Nicene Creed that Jesus "will come again in glory to judge the living and the dead, and his kingdom will have no end." As Christians we look to the future. We live in the world but are not to be of the world.

How do you think Mary's example can help us to prepare for the second coming of Christ?

Madonna and Child

165

different from any other New Testament book. Nevertheless this book is part of the inspired word of God and must be looked at carefully.

Revelation is an apocalyptic book. From your study of literary forms in the Bible, you know that *apocalyptic writing* is highly symbolic and that it uses rich images to describe future times and the end of the world. In attempting to describe the last moments of world history, this type of writing refers to imaginary catastrophes and a struggle in which God finally destroys the forces of evil. Apocalyptic writings are statements of faith wrapped in symbols. They usually include descriptions of the heavenly throne room, grotesque figures with animal features, series of numbers and calculations, cosmic battle scenes, earthquakes, lightning, and storms. This type of writing is certainly not dull!

Like all writers who used this form, the author of Revelation loved symbols, especially numbers. For example, the number *four* stood for the world, the number *six* stood for imperfection, and the number *one thousand* stood for endlessness.

Filled with Symbols

On a street corner in your town or on television, you may have seen people carrying posters announcing "The end is near" or "Jesus is coming soon." Where do these people get such ideas? Why do their beliefs seem so different from ours?

People who expect that the end of the world will happen in the near future often get their ideas from a misunderstanding of one special book in the New Testament, the Book of Revelation. This book is the last book of the Bible. Anyone who has looked at it even briefly knows that it is much

Seven is another important number. Remember that seven is a symbol for completeness or perfection. The author addresses seven letters to the Churches of Asia Minor (Revelation 2:1—3:22). After depicting God's heavenly throne and Christ as the Lamb, the author has the Lamb open seven seals (Revelation 6:1—8:1), and the angels blow on seven trumpets and pour out seven bowls of God's fury upon the earth (Revelation 16:1–21). The book closes with God's triumph over Babylon, the symbol of pagan Rome, and the appearance of the new Jerusalem. And these are just a few of the symbols that are part of the Book of Revelation.

Getting to the Truth

After encountering some of the unusual features found in the Book of Revelation, it is easy to see why some people are afraid to read it or avoid it out of frustration. Catholics, however, need not fear this book. Guided by the teaching authority of the Church and faithful Scripture scholars, a Catholic reading of Revelation takes into account the literary form of the work, its original setting in history, and its message of faith.

The Book of Revelation was written as a response to persecution in the early Church. It is often dated around A.D. 95 during the reign of the Roman emperor Domitian. Christians, like all the other citizens of the Roman Empire, were expected to worship the emperor as a god. In fact Domitian liked to be called "my lord and my god." But worshiping the emperor would have been impossible for a faithful follower of Christ. That is why the Book of Revelation refers to Christ the Lamb, and not to the emperor, as the "Lord our God" (Revelation 4:11).

The emperor, in fact, is referred to as a beast. So also is one of his officials in Asia Minor, who at that time was promoting the worship of the emperor. The official is described by the author this way: "Then I saw another beast come up out of the earth; it had two horns like a lamb's but spoke like a dragon. It wielded all the authority of the first beast in its sight and made the earth and its inhabitants worship the first beast" (Revelation 13:11–12). It is no wonder that Christians feared such beastlike pagan officials who had the power to make them suffer or even put them to death.

Some people have said that the Book of Revelation was written in code language and has to be decoded by people in later ages. Nothing could be further from the truth. The message of Revelation was symbolic but crystal clear to its first readers and remains so today. The message of this inspired book is this: Through the death and resurrection of Jesus, God has been victorious over sin and death. Even in the midst of persecution and other hardships, Christians have no reason to fear but should be strong in professing their faith. They will be victorious over all their persecutors in the end, just as they were over the Romans. Even in the midst of trials and testing of faith, the author of this book could write:

> Then I heard a loud voice in heaven say:
> "Now have salvation and power come,
>   and the kingdom of our God
>   and the authority of his Anointed."
> Revelation 12:10

 Read the following acclamations of Christ found in Revelation and make them part of your prayer this week: 1:4–7 and 19:6–7.

Scripture Insight

The Book of Revelation has another name. It is sometimes called the Apocalypse, from the Greek word meaning "revelation." The author of this book calls himself John (1:4). He had been exiled to the island of Patmos, a Roman penal colony. Although he never claimed to be John the apostle and evangelist, he is sometimes identified as that New Testament person. Perhaps he was a disciple of John the apostle.

Pilgrims of Hope

With the assurance of Jesus' death and resurrection and God's victory over sin and death, Christians can live as people of hope. With the virtue of *hope,* we trust in the promises of Christ, whose resurrection gives us the assurance that death will be overcome by life, that goodness will conquer evil, and that we will be saved and blessed with the fullness of life. As people of hope, we look forward to the second coming of Christ, but we do not worry about his coming.

People of hope never stop believing in all of life's possibilities, no matter what. They remember always, even in periods of hardship and suffering, that God loves them and wants what is best for them. During times of discouragement they never surrender or give in to defeat. Rather, they continue to aspire to what is best, especially the goodness and glory of God. This was the attitude of the author of the Book of Revelation and of the authors of the rest of the New Testament as well.

Being hopeful people makes us a pilgrim people, a pilgrim Church, a people on the way, waiting for fulfillment of the kingdom. Paul realized what it meant to be a part of this pilgrim people. It meant that he had to work hard to bring the good news of Christ to others. Paul wrote about this to the Church in Corinth:

> All this I do for the sake of the gospel, so that I too may have a share in it. Do you not know that the runners in the stadium all run in the race, but only one wins the prize? Run so as to win. Every athlete exercises discipline in every way. They do it to win a perishable crown, but we an imperishable one. Thus I do not run aimlessly; I do not fight as if I were shadowboxing. No, I drive my body and train it, for fear that, after having preached to others, I myself should be disqualified.
> 1 Corinthians 9:23–27

Evangelizers of Hope

The earliest Christian communities have given us a marvelous example of the way we should be acting today. They realized that they did not invent their faith but that they received it. The same is true for us today. We must once again proclaim in our day the words and actions of Jesus of Nazareth. We must take up the gospels again and reread the word of God. Only in this way can we be evangelizers, sharers of the good news that the world must hear.

Is evangelization simply sharing information about Jesus? Not at all. It involves a real communication of faith and an invitation to change one's life and turn to the Lord. One of the greatest examples of evangelization can be found in the life of Saint Francis of Assisi. As a young man he dreamed of being a knight in shining armor. But very soon he saw the horrors of war and violence, and his dream faded and grew sour. He searched and searched to find true meaning in his life and in his faith. Then God touched his life and began to prepare Francis for a life of evangelization. What would Francis do? The message was clear to him when he heard the words of the gospel, "If you wish to be perfect, go, sell what you have and give to [the] poor, and you will have treasure in heaven. Then come, follow me" (Matthew 19:21).

Francis did just that. He took seriously the words of the gospel and changed his life forever. He patterned his life on Christ's life. The challenge is there for each of us, too. We may not have to be as radical as Francis. Yet, we need to have the same spirit that he had, the same spirit that is part of each saint's life—to take the gospel seriously. If we could all act in the same way, we could change the world and truly be evangelizers of hope.

What do you think gave Francis of Assisi the courage to follow the words of the gospel?

Saint Francis of Assisi, an evangelizer of hope

CATHOLIC ID

When Catholics stand at Mass for the proclamation of the gospel, they often trace the cross on the forehead, the lips, and the heart. This gesture reminds us that the gospel is to fill our mind, be ever on our lips, and be always in our hearts. What a great reminder for us to be evangelizers of hope!

Some Final Words

This has been a challenging course in the study of the New Testament. As we look back, it may seem that we have covered many topics and learned many things. That is true. However, we have really only scratched the surface. We have been given some of the tools and some of the important insights we will need to spend a lifetime with the New Testament.

Before we conclude our study, there are several ideas that need to be repeated. The first is that the New Testament is timeless. Even though the world has changed many times since the days of Jesus and the early Church, the message of the New Testament remains the same. It needs to be applied in each generation and in each culture throughout the world, respecting the dignity of different peoples. But the message never changes. It is the message that Jesus is the Savior of the world and that he has come to set us free.

Another very important idea to remember is that mistaken interpretations of the New Testament have occurred in the history of the Church, especially when people have forgotten to do the hard work of study and reflection. Ugly things have been done in the name of Scripture. Forgetting that the Bible is the Church's book, some people have tried to eliminate the Church's role in interpreting it; some have even tried to eliminate the Church itself. Others have denied Jesus' humanity, and some have even denied his divinity in the name of the New Testament! Still others have promoted a hatred of people who are not Christians. Consider, for example, the serious sin of anti-Semitism, the wrongful discrimination against Jews. All this shows us the need to listen to the Holy Spirit, who guides the community of the Church in its ongoing life.

The author of the Letter to the Hebrews wrote, "Jesus Christ is the same yesterday, today, and forever. Do not be carried away by all kinds of strange teaching" (13:8–9). What a wonderful truth this is for us to think about in our nonstop, technological world. Jesus and the message he brought to the world never change.

If we could be transported back in time to the earliest Christian communities in Corinth or Ephesus or Jerusalem or Rome, what would it be like? If we could meet the earliest Christians and with them hear for the first time the New Testament letters and gospels, would we feel at home in these communities? Absolutely! We would realize right away that we proclaim the same loving Father, the same Lord Jesus, and the same Holy Spirit, the Spirit who gives the Church its life in every age.

Perhaps the challenge that we face today in a world of instant communication and limitless travel is a challenge that never before faced the Christian community. It is a challenge for us to be in love with God's word so that this word enters into every part of the human experience. Only in this way will we make progress in being true brothers and sisters in Christ. As we do this, we will be able to understand the words of Paul to the Ephesians and make them our own prayer:

I kneel before the Father, from whom every family in heaven and on earth is named, that he may grant you in accord with the riches of his glory to be strengthened with power through his Spirit in the inner self, and that Christ may dwell in your hearts through faith; that you, rooted and grounded in love, may have strength to comprehend with all the holy ones what is the breadth and length and height and depth, and to know the love of Christ that surpasses knowledge, so that you may be filled with the fullness of God.

Now to him who is able to accomplish far more than all we ask or imagine, by the power at work within us, to him be glory in the church and in Christ Jesus to all generations, forever and ever. Amen.
Ephesians 3:14–21

Catholic Teachings

About Evangelization
In 1975 Pope Paul VI wrote some memorable words about evangelization. He said, "Evangelization is the grace and vocation proper to the Church, her deepest identity. She exists in order to evangelize" (*Announcing the Gospel*, 14).

The Colosseum, Rome, Italy, one of many places where Christians gave witness to Jesus with their lives

things to think about

What do you think is the most important thing we can learn about the Blessed Virgin Mary in the New Testament?

What relationship did Jesus want us to have with his mother?

things to share

If someone told you that the end of the world was going to happen very soon, what would you say?

Some Catholics have a tough time with the Book of Revelation and avoid it. Knowing what you do about this book, how could you help these people to appreciate it more?

WORDS TO REMEMBER

Find and define the following:

second coming _____
_____
_____

apocalyptic writing _____
_____
_____

OnLine
WITH THE PARISH

Many parishes publish in their bulletins the Scripture readings for the following Sunday liturgies. Take time each week to read the Scripture passages that will be proclaimed on that day. See how much more you will get out of the readings by making this a weekly practice.

1. What is the difference between the first and second comings of Jesus to the world?

2. What is the significance of Mary's yes to the angel?

3. Does anyone know when the second coming will occur? Explain.

4. Why was the Book of Revelation written? Why does it use so many symbols?

5. Why should Christians be people of hope?

Life in the Spirit

We do not have to wait until Sunday to pray with Sacred Scripture. We can choose a passage each day and make it part of our prayer. When you open the Scriptures, you may want to do so in the presence of a crucifix. In this way you can remember the words of the New Testament that remind us to do this "while keeping our eyes fixed on Jesus" (Hebrews 12:2).

CHAPTER 15

Jesus Christ In Every Age

For Christ plays in ten thousand places,
Lovely in limbs, and lovely in eyes not his
To the Father through the features
of men's faces.

Gerard Manley Hopkins, S.J.

Who do you say that I am?

Luke 9:20

During this course you have learned many things about Jesus Christ, but there is still so much more to learn! Understanding Jesus and becoming his follower are the work of a lifetime.

One thing we do not know about him is his physical appearance. No description of his looks is given in Scripture. Perhaps that is fortunate because it allows each culture and race and age to find his image in their own people.

"Who do you say that I am?" Jesus asked his disciples. Imagine that Jesus asks that question of you. What would your answer be? Who is Jesus for you? When you pray, what name do you give him? Savior? brother? judge? friend? When you picture him, what image comes to your mind?

Take a minute to jot down any words or phrases that express Jesus for you.

Now we will examine the ways artists of many ages and different cultures responded in art to these questions. You will soon see that there is a great variety of responses. Each generation seems to find in Jesus a way to answer the important questions of its time. In this chapter you will be looking at images of Jesus through the ages by many artists and hearing the words of Scripture that motivated their work. Look and listen, and let the words of the gospels come alive for you.

Totem Cross
Peters, 20th century

The totem poles of the Pacific Northwest serve much the same purpose as the wayside crosses in rural Europe. This artist combined the two traditions, placing Jesus on a totem cross to stress that he belongs, not to a single people, but to the world.

Crucifixion
Chagall, 20th century

Jesus was a Jew, and Chagall, also a Jew, paints the crucifixion in a world that knows the horrors of the Nazi death camps.

Mount Calvary
Johnson, c.1944

This very original work comes out of the tradition of the African American community. The painter makes the figures dark-skinned to show that Jesus belongs to the black world just as much as to the white world.

A savior has been born for you who is Messiah and Lord.

Luke 2:11

Artists have always been fascinated with the least-known period of Jesus' life: his infancy and childhood. Perhaps because so much is left to the imagination and to faith, the interpretations of the child Jesus seem unlimited and highly personal. Artists often depict him as a member of their own race.

✚ Do you have a favorite image or picture of the Christ child? Describe it.

Now listen as a member of your group reads Luke 2:1–14. How do you feel the different pieces of art on these pages reflect the gospel account?

Madonna and Child
African, 20th century

In this wooden carving an African artist gives Jesus and Mary African features and dresses them in traditional clothing.

The Adoration of the Shepherds
De LaTour, 17th century

Mary, Joseph, and the shepherds wear the clothes of French peasants.

The Passover in the Holy Family
Rossetti, 1856

The artist paints the Holy Family preparing, as religious Jews, for the feast of Passover. He even includes Jesus' cousin, the young John the Baptist.

Hopi Virgin and Child 2
Giuliani, 20th century

The artist portrays a Native American Mary and Jesus wearing traditional Hopi clothes.

Read Luke 2:41–52.
Christ Returning from the Temple with his Parents, Rembrandt, 1654

In this etching the artist depicts Jesus, Mary, and Joseph returning to Nazareth from Jerusalem.

✝ *If you were able to paint or carve an image of the child Jesus, what would you want to show?*

179

The words I have spoken to you are spirit and life.

John 6:63

The pictures on these pages show artists' interpretations of Jesus in his ministry of teaching, the main work of his public life. See how each artist depicts Jesus from his own vantage point, artistic style, religious understanding, and culture. Take time to look up and read aloud the Scripture account that each artist portrays.

✝ What words of Jesus give you "spirit and life"? If you were an artist, what teaching of Jesus would you wish to portray? Explain your choice.

Read John 10:14–16.

The Good Shepherd
late 3rd century

This ivory carving is the earliest figure of Jesus we have. The artist depicts him as a young, gentle, Good Shepherd.

Read John 4:4–30.

The Woman of Samaria
William Dyce, 1806–1864

A weary Jesus asks a Samaritan woman for a drink. In return he offers her "living water." The artist captures the moment just before Jesus changes her life forever.

Read Mark 10:13–16.

Let the Children Come to Me
Fritz von Uhde, 1884

Uhde, a Dutch artist, places Jesus in a Dutch schoolroom. The artist wanted the children of his time to understand Jesus' love for them.

Read Luke 10:38–42.

Christ in the House of Martha and Mary
Jan Vermeer, c.1654–1656

Vermeer pictures Jesus at the home of Martha and Mary. Mary sits listening to Jesus, totally absorbed in him, while Martha complains that she is doing all the work. What do you think Jesus is saying to her?

Read John 13:31–35.

Detail from a Byzantine mosaic in Hagia Sophia
12th century

This Byzantine mosaic shows a serious, thoughtful Jesus in the act of teaching.

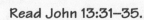

Who then is this whom even wind and sea obey?

Mark 4:41

The Scripture accounts of the miraculous works done by Jesus have always provided artists with dramatic and appealing subjects. In the paintings shown on these pages, the artists often place Jesus in the landscape or setting of their own country.

Look at each painting as the gospel passage is read. What qualities of Christ does each artist portray? his power? compassion? transcendence?

Read Matthew 20:29–34.

Jesus Healing the Blind of Jericho
Poussin, 17th century

The gospel often mentions that Jesus touched those he cured. The artist portrays the moment when "moved with pity, Jesus touched their eyes."

✚ Choose a favorite miracle account from the gospels. How would you paint the scene as if it were happening today?

Read Luke 8:40–56.

The Raising of Jairus' Daughter
George Percy Jacomb-Hood,
1857–1927

A curious crowd, believing
that Jesus has arrived too
late to save the girl, jams the
doorway, trying to get a view of
what Jesus will do. He stands
serenely, and says simply,
"Child, arise!" The painter
captures the moment just
before he speaks.

Read John 6:1–14.

Miracle of the Loaves and Fishes
Giovanni Lanfranco, 1582–1647

The artist shows Jesus at the moment
when the loaves and fishes that he has
blessed are being distributed by the
disciples to the huge crowd.

Read Mark 4:35–41.

The Stilling of the Tempest
Ho-Peh, 1950s

A contemporary Chinese artist paints a Chinese
Jesus calming the storm. This is another example
of the universal appeal of Jesus.

Blessed are those who have not seen and have believed.

John 20:29

The early Christians did not have many images of Christ. Perhaps that is because in times of persecution it would have placed them in danger. The religious images used in the early Church were symbols such as a fish or a lamb or a laurel wreath. The earliest image we have of Christ is the Good Shepherd carving from the third century (see page 180).

It was not until the fourth century that the cross began to appear in Christian art. After that we begin to see many other events of Christ's life depicted.

What images of Jesus do you feel our world needs to see today? Write or sketch your response here.

Read John 19: 30.

Head of Jesus, detail from
Christ on the Cross
Diego Velazquez, 1599–1660

The great Spanish painter shows Jesus at the moment he "bowed his head" and died.

Read Luke 24:13–32.

The Supper at Emmaus
Diego Velazquez, 1599–1660

As Jesus blesses the bread, the disciples turn to each other in their dawning recognition that it is truly the Lord. The two men are in shadow; Jesus is about to disappear into the light. How does the artist portray the bewildered and joyful amazement of the disciples?

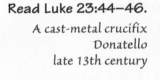

Read John 20:24–29.

Incredulity of Saint Thomas,
Rubens, 17th century

His unbelief giving way to belief, the doubting Thomas gazes in wonder at the wounds of Jesus. What would you say Jesus' face expresses?

Read Luke 23:44–46.

A cast-metal crucifix
Donatello
late 13th century

185

BLESSED BE THE LORD,
THE GOD OF ISRAEL;

he has come to his people and set them free.

He has raised up for us a mighty savior,
born of the house of his servant David.

Through his holy prophets he promised
of old,
that he would save us from our enemies,
from the hands of all who hate us.

He promised to show mercy to our fathers
and to remember his holy covenant.

This was the oath he swore to our father
Abraham:
to set us free from the hands of our
enemies,
free to worship him without fear,
holy and righteous in his sight all the days
of our life.

You, my child, shall be called the prophet
of the Most High;
for you will go before the Lord to prepare
his way,
to give his people knowledge of salvation
by the forgiveness of their sins.

In the tender compassion of our God
the dawn from on high shall break upon us,
to shine on those who dwell in darkness
and the shadow of death,
and to guide our feet into the way of peace.

Luke 1:68–79
CANTICLE OF ZECHARIAH
(THE BENEDICTUS)

MY SOUL PROCLAIMS
THE GREATNESS OF THE LORD,

my spirit rejoices in God my Savior;
for he has looked with favor on his lowly
servant.

From this day all generations will call me
blessed:
the Almighty has done great things for me,
and holy is his Name.

He has mercy on those who fear him
in every generation.

He has shown the strength of his arm,
he has scattered the proud in their conceit.

He has cast down the mighty from their
thrones,
and has lifted up the lowly.

He has filled the hungry with good things,
and the rich he has sent away empty.

He has come to the help of his servant Israel
for he has remembered his promise of mercy,
the promise he made to our fathers,
to Abraham and his children for ever.

Luke 1:46–55
CANTICLE OF MARY (THE MAGNIFICAT)

LORD,
NOW YOU LET YOUR SERVANT GO IN PEACE;

your word has been fulfilled:
my own eyes have seen the salvation
which you have prepared in the sight
of every people:

a light to reveal you to the nations
and the glory of your people Israel.

Luke 2:29–32
CANTICLE OF SIMEON (NUNC DIMITTIS)

PRAYER & PRAISE

[CHRIST] IS THE IMAGE
OF THE INVISIBLE GOD,

the firstborn of all creation.
For in him were created all things in
    heaven and on earth,
    the visible and the invisible,
    whether thrones or dominions or
    principalities or powers;
    all things were created through him
    and for him.
He is before all things,
    and in him all things hold together.
He is the head of the body, the church.
He is the beginning, the firstborn from
    the dead,
    that in all things he himself might be
    preeminent.
For in him all the fullness was pleased to
    dwell,
and through him to reconcile all things
    for him,
making peace by the blood of his cross
[through him], whether those on earth or
    those in heaven.

Colossians 1:15–20
CANTICLE ON CHRIST

BLESSED BE THE GOD
AND FATHER OF OUR
LORD JESUS CHRIST,

who has blessed us in Christ with every
spiritual blessing in the heavens, as he chose
us in him, before the foundation of the
world, to be holy and without blemish
before him. In love he destined us for
adoption to himself through Jesus Christ,
in accord with the favor of his will, for the
praise of the glory of his grace that he
granted us in the beloved.

Ephesians 1:3–6
SPIRITUAL BLESSINGS IN CHRIST

IF I SPEAK IN HUMAN
AND ANGELIC TONGUES

but do not have love, I am a resounding gong
or a clashing cymbal. And if I have the gift of
prophecy and comprehend all mysteries and
all knowledge; if I have all faith so as to move
mountains, but do not have love, I am
nothing. If I give away everything I own, and
if I hand my body over so that I may boast
but do not have love, I gain nothing.

Love is patient, love is kind. It is not jealous,
[love] is not pompous, it is not inflated, it is
not rude, it does not seek its own interests,
it is not quick-tempered, it does not brood
over injury, it does not rejoice over
wrongdoing but rejoices with the truth. It
bears all things, believes all things, hopes all
things, endures all things.

Love never fails. If there are prophecies, they
will be brought to nothing; if tongues, they
will cease; if knowledge, it will be brought
to nothing. For we know partially and we
prophesy partially, but when the perfect
comes, the partial will pass away. When I was
a child, I used to talk as a child, think as a
child, reason as a child; when I became a
man, I put aside childish things. At present
we see indistinctly, as in a mirror, but then
face to face. At present I know partially; then
I shall know fully, as I am fully known. So
faith, hope, love remain, these three; but
the greatest of these is love.

1 Corinthians 13:1–13
PAUL'S WORDS ON LOVE

THOUGH [JESUS] WAS IN THE FORM OF GOD,

[he] did not regard equality with God
  something to be grasped.
Rather, he emptied himself
  taking the form of a slave,
  coming in human likeness;
  and found human in appearance,
  he humbled himself,
  becoming obedient to death,
    even death on a cross.
Because of this, God greatly exalted him
  and bestowed on him the name
  that is above every name,
  that at the name of Jesus
  every knee should bend,
  of those in heaven and on earth
    and under the earth,
  and every tongue confess that
  Jesus Christ is Lord,
    to the glory of God the Father.

Philippians 2:6–11
CANTICLE FROM PHILIPPIANS

ASK AND IT WILL BE GIVEN TO YOU;

seek and you will find;
knock and the door will be opened to you.
For everyone who asks, receives;
and the one who seeks, finds;
and to the one who knocks,
the door will be opened.

Matthew 7:7–8
THE ANSWER TO PRAYERS

PUT ON THEN, AS GOD'S CHOSEN ONES,

holy and beloved, heartfelt compassion, kindness, humility, gentleness, and patience, bearing with one another and forgiving one another, if one has a grievance against another; as the Lord has forgiven you, so must you also do. And over all these put on love, that is, the bond of perfection. And let the peace of Christ control your hearts, the peace into which you were also called in one body. And be thankful. Let the word of Christ dwell in you richly, as in all wisdom you teach and admonish one another, singing psalms, hymns, and spiritual songs with gratitude in your hearts to God. And whatever you do, in word or in deed, do everything in the name of the Lord Jesus, giving thanks to God the Father through him.

Colossians 3:12–17
THE CHRISTIAN LIFE

GOD IS LOVE, AND WHOEVER REMAINS

in love remains in God and God in him. In this is love brought to perfection among us, that we have confidence on the day of judgment because as he is, so are we in this world. There is no fear in love, but perfect love drives out fear because fear has to do with punishment, and so one who fears is not yet perfect in love. We love because he first loved us. If anyone says, "I love God," but hates his brother, he is a liar; for whoever does not love a brother whom he has seen cannot love God whom he has not seen. This is the commandment we have from him: whoever loves God must also love his brother.

1 John 4:16–21
GOD IS LOVE

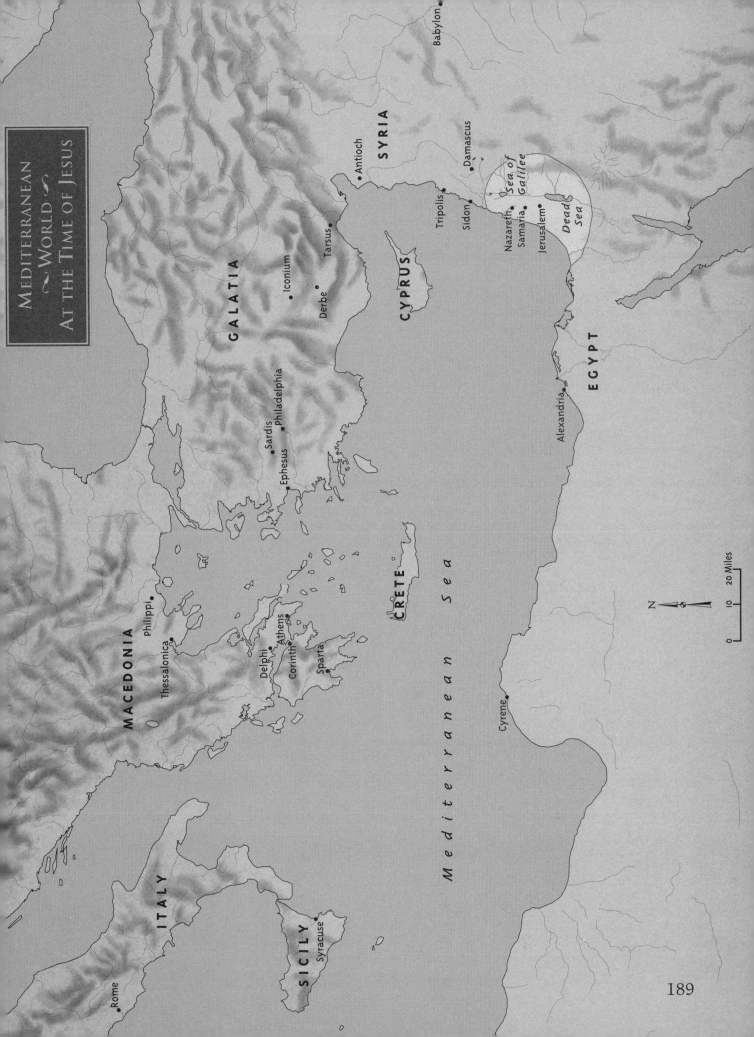

MEDITERRANEAN
WORLD
AT THE TIME OF JESUS

SYRIA

Babylon

Antioch

Damascus

CYPRUS

Tripolis
Sidon

Sea of
Galilee

Nazareth
Samaria
Jerusalem

Dead
Sea

GALATIA

Iconium

Derbe

Tarsus

EGYPT

Alexandria

Sardis
Philadelphia

Ephesus

MACEDONIA

Philippi

Thessalonica

Delphi
Athens
Corinth
Sparta

CRETE

Cyrene

Mediterranean Sea

N

20 Miles

10

0

ITALY

SICILY

Syracuse

Rome

189

Index

Abba, 59, *98*, 164
Abraham, 34, 38, 44, 47, 53, 56, 62, 84, 86, 94, 95, 141
Acts of the Apostles, 21, 74, 141, 146, 147, 154
Alpha and Omega, 94, 95, 100
Anointing with oil, ritual of, 49, 154
Apocalypse, *See* Revelation.
Apocalyptic writing, *39, 166*
Apostles (the Twelve), 12, 13, 34, 35, 59, 69, 98, 131–135, *141*–146, 154
 call of, 12, 34, 98, 141, 142
Apostolic leaders, 144, 145
Apostolic succession, 133
Aramaic, 58, 59, 72, 98
Ascension, 129, *135*, 144

Baptism, 83, 93, 99, 101, 121, 153, 154, 158
Beatification, *161*
Beatitudes, 71, *158*, 159
Bethlehem, 13, 44, 57, 84, 85
Bible, 11, 13, *14*, **18–29**, **30–41**, 68, 69, 104, 143, 157, 166, 167, 170, 173
 authorship, 20, 21, 25, 33, 35
 books of, 14, 15, 20, 27, 97
 inspiration theories, 22, 23
 literary forms, *36–39*, 72, 166, 167
 translations, 37
 word of God, 21, 26, 32, 36, 37
Bishop(s), 145, 147
Blessed Trinity, 93, 121, 122, 158, 164, 165
Body and Blood of Christ, 47, 49, 129, 132, 154

Canon of Scripture, 27
Catechism of the Catholic Church, 9, 14, 21, 25, 27, 83, 99, 119, 133, 135, 153, 159
Catholic(s), 9, 14, 21, 23, 24, 39, 61, 68, 119–121, 128, 132, 165, 167, 169
Chrism, 49
Christian(s), 10, 13, 153, 156–158, 164, 165, 167, 168
 early, 10, 11, 13, 14, 154, 184
 people of faith, 12, 25, 105, 110, 135, 164
 people of hope, 168
 pilgrim people, 168
 temples of the Holy Spirit, 153

Christmas, 74, 85, 88, 128
Church, 9, 12–14, 23, 24, 27, 33, 34, 37, 39, 63, 69, 73, 75, 81, 111, 119, 123, **138–149**, *144*, **150–161**, 165
 apostolic foundations, 135, 141, 143, 145, 146
 apostolic ministries, 135, 142, 145, 146
 Catholic, 13, 14, 21–23, 26
 Church of Christ, 144, 147, 152
 community, 12, 13, 24, 119, 153, 154, 170
 early, 12, 13, 24, 27, 35, 37, 38, 59, 61, 72, 80, 84, 142–144, 146, 147, 154, 155, 165, 167, 170, 184
 members, 9, 121, 135, 153, 154, 157–159
 origin, 140, 141
Church, images, 152, 153
 body of Christ, 147, 153, 155
 bride of Christ, 153
 God's building, 153
 household of God, 153
 light of the world, 153
 one loaf, 153
 people of God, 141, 144, 153
 salt of the earth, 151, 153
 sheepfold, 153
 temple of the Holy Spirit, 153
 vine and the branches, 153
Commandment, *See* New Commandment.
Communion of saints, *157*
Covenant, 14, 46–48, 50, 51, 126
 biblical, *46*
 new, 47–49, 129, 132, 133, 141, 144
 old, 49, 129, 141
 political, *46*

Deacon(s), 145
Dead Sea, 56, 59, 83
Disciples, 12, 71, 72, 93, 94, 98, 108, 131, 132, 134, 135, 141–143, 156, 158, 165, 185
Divine inspiration, *21*–24, 25, 27, 32, 104
Divine revelation, 13, 24, *33*

Easter, 74
Elizabeth, 80, 81
Emmaus, 135, 185
Epistles, *38*, 69, 155

Eucharist, 16, 99, 101, 111, 132, 133, 137, 146, 153–155
 Body and Blood of the Lord, 47, 49, 129, 132, 154
 Bread of Life, 99
 celebration of, *See* Mass.
 real presence, 154
 sacrament of sacraments, 153
 sacrifice of the cross, 51, 129, 132, 133
Evangelists, *69*, 71, 77, 81, 84, 86, 106
 symbols of, 72–75
Evangelization, 111, *145*, 169, 171

Faith, 9, 32, 105, 106, 111, 135, 156, 167
 mystery of, 25, 134
 people of, 12, 25, 105, 110, 135, 164
 practice of, 9, 156, 157, 159
 profession of, 37, 71, 167
 truths of, 26, 121
Francis of Assisi, 85, 169

Galilee, 44, 57, 58
Genealogy, *38*, 73, 84, *86*, 87
God, 34, 44, 50, 51, 132, 153, 166, 167
 Abba, 59, *98*, 164
 author of the Bible, 21, 22, 27
 communion with, 133, 158
 creator, 93
 faithful to promises, 44, 45, 47
 forgiveness, 96, 99, 116, 117, 120
 grace, 120, 121, 157
 law of, 50, 51, 59, 63, 118, 131
 Lord, 50, 99, 118, 141
 love and care, 61, 99, 116–118, 120, 121, 156
 mercy, 96, 109, 110, 116, 117, 120
 mystery, 99
 one true, 46, 47, 50, 61, 93
 plan of, 86, 140, 141
 power, 105, 107, 108, 121
 presence, 50, 51
 promise of, 38, 47, 82, 85
 providence, *121*
 relationship with, 9, 46, 47
 revelation, 24, 99
Trinity of Persons, 93
 God the Father, 25, 29, 59, 87, 93, 94, 98, 99, 106, 110, 121, 129, 131, 133, 142, 146, 153, 155, 164, 165, 171

Italicized numbers refer to definitions   **Bold-faced** numbers refer to chapters